BIRNBAUM'S

2019

P9-CEV-615

Walt Disney World®

For Kids

THE OFFICIAL GUIDE

Wendy Lefkon
Editorial Director

Jill Safro
Editor

Jennie Hess
Contributing Editor

Clark Wakabayashi
Designer

Alexandra Mayes Birnbaum
Consulting Editor

Disney
EDITIONS

LOS ANGELES · NEW YORK

For Steve, who made all of this possible.

ISBN 978-1-368-01934-7
FAC-038091-18215
First Edition, September 2018
10 9 8 7 6 5 4 3 2 1

The Official Disney Fan Club

D23.com

Printed in the United States of America

An enormous debt of gratitude is owed to Jessica Ward, Diane Hodges, Jerry Gonzalez,
Jennifer Eastwood, Monica Vasquez, Pam Brandon, Geoffrey Cook, Steven Miller,
Elisabeth Hurkes, Todd Heiden, Terry Brinkoetter, Jackie Vernon, Andrea Wolowitz,
and Karen McClintock for making this book possible. On the cover photography team
we want to thank Mike Carroll, Stacey Cook, Lori Loftis, Irene Ferdinand, Mickey
Mouse, and Minnie Mouse, all of whom performed above and beyond the call of duty.
And to Phil Lengyel, Tom Elrod, Linda Warren, Bob Miller, and Charlie Ridgway, thanks
for believing in this project in the first place.

Other 2019 Birnbaum's Official Disney Guides:
Disneyland and *Walt Disney World*

SUSTAINABLE FORESTRY INITIATIVE — Certified Sourcing
www.sfiprogram.org
SFI-00993
Logo Applies to Text Stock Only

Contents

You're Going to DISNEY WORLD!

When you first heard the news, you couldn't believe your ears. Could it be true? Were you really going on a vacation to Walt Disney World? Well, believe it or not, it's true! Before you know it, you'll be in the sunny state of Florida. It's the home of Walt Disney World and the most famous mouse on planet Earth. (Hint: His name starts with M.)

If you have ever been there, you already know that it's one mighty big place with lots to do. In fact, there is so much going on that it can get a little confusing. That's where this book comes in handy. It describes everything in the World, from the Magic Kingdom theme park to the Hoop-Dee-Doo Musical Revue. And it's filled with advice from kids like you.

There is no right or wrong way to read this book. You can start on the first page and read straight through to the end. Or you can skip around, read your favorite parts first, and come back to the rest later.

No matter what you do, one thing is for sure: When you are done, you will be a true-blue Disney expert. Soon folks may start asking YOU for advice on how to have the most awesome vacation at Walt Disney World!

Pack a Pen and
Take Me Along With You

Don't leave this book behind when you head for the parks. It's full of tips and information that you'll want to remember. There are pages for photos and autographs, too — so don't forget to bring a pen and your camera. Here are some ways to use this book while visiting the wonderful world of Disney:

Track Your Trip

Each time you check out an attraction, check it off in this book. Then you'll know what's left to see on your next visit.

Search for Hidden Mickeys

Disney Imagineers have hidden images of Mickey Mouse all over Walt Disney World. (Many look like the three connected circles that form Mickey's head.) You might see them in shadows, lights, drawings, or even in the clouds at some attractions. Look in this book for each **HIDDEN MICKEY ALERT!** to find a clue. Keep track of the number of Hidden Mickeys that you discover. When your Walt Disney World trip is over, write that number on page 141 of this book's Magical Memories section.

Find the Fastpass

FP+

Would you like to go to the front of the line at some of the best rides? You can if you have a **Fastpass+** selection. They are offered for every ride that has a Fastpass+ symbol by its name in this book. Here's how it works: Reserve a Fastpass with the My Disney Experience app or website (ask a parent for help). You may also get a same-day Fastpass at a station in each park — get there early! Visit the attraction at your assigned time, and soon you should be on the ride. It is free for all guests — as long as they have a park ticket.

We're Warning You!

Disney rides are full of surprises. That's part of what makes them so much fun. But not everyone likes surprises. So if things like loud noises or fast turns scare you, look at the book's ATTRACTION REACTION warnings before you go on each ride. That way, the only surprises you come across will be good ones!

The last pages of this book are for autographs.

Meet the Readers

What do the kids who helped with this book all have in common? They love Walt Disney World! How do we know? They told us so! Every kid who wrote to us last year received a survey form. The surveys came back filled with opinions about Walt Disney World. The forms also helped us find out about readers' interests and backgrounds.

What did we learn? For starters, a whole lot of you enjoy reading, writing, playing sports, making music, and computers. You also like dancing, singing, and drawing. Your favorite Walt Disney World hotels are Port Orleans Riverside, Polynesian Village, and Beach Club. You're not all crazy about dark or scary rides. But wild rides like Big Thunder Mountain and Splash Mountain are at the top of your list. You think Blizzard Beach is the perfect place to splash around. And when you can't find a Mickey Mouse ice cream bar to snack on, you love popcorn, Mickey-shaped pretzels, a turkey leg, or a frozen pineapple treat called Dole Whip. Yum!

To everyone who filled out a survey, THANK YOU! This book couldn't have been written without you.

— Jill Safro, Editor

Mickey is Number One!

It's probably not a surprise to hear that Mickey Mouse is still the most popular Disney character with readers. And his best girl, Minnie, is in second place. But who would have guessed that Goofy would be a close third? Gawrsh! Rounding out the top five faves are Donald and Pluto. Who's your favorite? Let us know!

The Magic Kingdom Rules!

More than half of our readers picked the Magic Kingdom as their favorite theme park. Is it yours?

Animal Kingdom 6%

Epcot 13%

Disney's Hollywood Studios 15%

Magic Kingdom 66%

You Love a Wild Ride!

We asked you what types of rides you like best. It turns out most of you like the twists and turns of thrill rides. What daredevils!

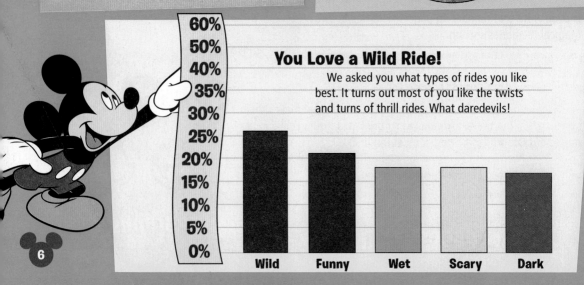

Look for this Reader Pleaser ribbon throughout the book. We've placed it beside our readers' 15 favorite Disney attractions. If you'd like to cast your vote for next year's Reader Pleasers, write us a letter and we'll send you a survey form. Our address is listed below.

The Reader Review

Every reader who was mailed a survey also got an application to become a Birnbaum Ace Reporter. Their Reader Reviews appear at the many attractions in this book. Use the opinions of the Ace Reporters to decide if the ride is worth the wait or one to skip!

And the Winner is . . .

One lucky Ace Reporter was picked at random to win a special prize. And the winner is . . . Samantha from Chicago, Illinois!

Samantha is 8 years old. Her favorite Walt Disney World attractions are Test Track and The Barnstormer. Who's on top of her favorite character list? That would be Donald Duck and Belle. Samantha enjoys drawing, Irish dancing, and playing softball. She loves to read, too! And when it comes to Walt Disney World hotels, she's a big fan of the Contemporary resort.

Way to go, Samantha! Thanks for your valuable input to the 2019 edition of Birnbaum's *Walt Disney World For Kids*.

READER TIP

Keep an eye out for this symbol. Every time you spot it, you'll find a great tip sent in by a reader. Do you have any Walt Disney World tips? We would love to hear them!

Meet the Editor

PHOTO BY MIKE CARROLL

Hi. My name's Jill. I'm one of the big kids who helped put this book together. Mickey and Minnie helped us out, too!

What do YOU think?

Do you agree or disagree with any of the kids in this book? Tell us! Send us a letter about your trip and a self-addressed, stamped envelope to the address on the right.

We will send you a survey and read every letter before we write next year's book.

Birnbaum's Disney Guides Kid Expert Applications

Disney Editions
125 West End Ave.
3rd floor
New York, NY 10023

Meet Walt Disney

Walt Disney was born in Illinois on December 5, 1901 — that's more than one hundred years ago! During his life and for all the years after, Walt Disney's company created famous cartoons, movies, theme parks, books, and toys (plus much, much more) for everyone to enjoy . . . but how did it all begin?

When Walt was a little boy, he would look up at the sky and imagine the clouds were animals. As the wind pushed a cloud, a pig would turn into a cow. Soon, the cow would become a chicken! It was then that Walt realized that anything was possible with a little imagination.

But he knew that success would not come from daydreaming alone. Growing up on a farm had taught him the importance of hard work. And it's a good thing, because without Walt's hard work, we would never have met the most famous mouse in the world.

Walt thought of Mickey as his own son.

Magical Milestones

1901
Walt Disney is born on December 5 in Chicago, Illinois.

1928
Walt creates Mickey Mouse. Mickey stars in the cartoon *Steamboat Willie.*

1937
Walt's animators finish *Snow White and the Seven Dwarfs,* the first full-length animated movie.

1955
Walt's dream to make a family theme park comes true. Disneyland opens in Anaheim.

1971
Walt Disney World (WDW) opens near Orlando, Florida.

1975
The first WDW roller coaster opens — Space Mountain!

1982
Epcot opens at WDW.

A mouse is born

In 1928, Walt created a little cartoon mouse. (Walt almost named him Mortimer Mouse. Luckily, Lilly Disney convinced her husband to name him Mickey Mouse instead!) Mickey's first movie was a black-and-white cartoon called *Steamboat Willie*. It was an instant success. But one hit wasn't enough for its creator. Walt was always looking for new challenges. In 1937, his animation company made the first full-length cartoon movie: *Snow White and the Seven Dwarfs*. Walt was very proud that he had made a movie for everyone in the family to enjoy. Family was very important to Walt. Every Saturday, he would do something special with his two daughters. They often went to an amusement park. The kids loved it, but Walt was sad that there weren't rides for parents. *I wish there were a place where children and grown-ups could have fun together*, he thought.

Steamboat Willie was the first talking cartoon ever made.

Mickey's birthday is November 18. When is yours?

A dream is a wish your heart makes

Since a place like that didn't exist, Walt decided to build it. At first he was going to call it Mickey Mouse Park, but then he named it Disneyland. Disneyland opened in Anaheim, California, in 1955. Families traveled from all over the world to visit it. Disneyland was so popular that Walt's new dream was to build an even bigger park: Disney World. He must have wished upon a star — because his dream came true.

1983 Tokyo Disneyland opens in the capital city of Japan.

1989 Disney's Hollywood Studios opens at WDW.

1992 Disneyland Paris opens in France.

1998 Disney's Animal Kingdom opens on Earth Day!

2014 Seven Dwarfs Mine Train chugs into the Magic Kingdom.

2016 Frozen Ever After opens in Epcot's Norway pavilion.

2018 Disney's Hollywood Studios welcomes Toy Story Land!

What a Wonderful World

Walt Disney loved dreaming up stories to tell and new ways to tell them. After he died, his brother Roy kept one of his biggest dreams alive. He made sure Walt's special "world" was built just the way Walt had imagined it. Roy even insisted that it be called *Walt* Disney World, so everyone would know it had been his brother's dream.

Walt Disney World officially opened on October 1, 1971. Since then, millions of people have stopped in for a visit. Some people come to Walt Disney World for a day, but most stay a little longer. There's just so much to see and do.

Pick a theme park, any theme park

The most famous part of Walt Disney World is the **Magic Kingdom**. It's home to Cinderella Castle, Splash Mountain, and those rascally Pirates of the Caribbean. It's also where you can have an adventure with Peter Pan or Winnie the Pooh. Kids of all ages can't get enough of this happy place. Of course, there are three other theme parks to see.

Epcot is a place of wonder and discovery. Here you can search for Nemo at The Seas with Nemo and Friends, ride the frosty Frozen Ever After attraction, and meet Anna and Elsa. It's also a great place to go on a "world tour" or design and test a speedy new car. Different countries have shops, restaurants, and attractions inside this park. Epcot opened in 1982.

Are you a showbiz fan? If so, you will get a kick out of **Disney's Hollywood Studios** theme park. It's filled with

movie and TV inspired rides and exhibits. The secrets of movie stunts are revealed at the Indiana Jones Epic Stunt Spectacular. C-3PO pilots guests on high-flying adventures at Star Tours — The Adventures Continue. And The Twilight Zone Tower of Terror scares *everybody* silly. Disney's Hollywood Studios opened in 1989.

Disney's Animal Kingdom celebrates the beauty of nature and the creatures that live in it. It got off to a roaring start in 1998. The park has what it takes to make any kid's day: an African safari ride with wild animals, dinosaurs that seem real, a roller coaster adventure with a scary abominable snowman, and a super slimy 3-D movie about bugs.

Chill out!

Need to cool off on a hot day? You can make a splash at a Disney water park. Between **Typhoon Lagoon** and **Blizzard Beach**, it's almost impossible to stay dry. Each one has slippery slides, tube rides, and some very cool pools.

But wait — there's more! Walt Disney World also has boats, bikes, and even horses to ride. It has hundreds of restaurants, shops, and other places to explore. In fact, no matter how many times you visit, there's always something new to see. Will Walt Disney World ever be finished? Not as long as there is imagination left in the world. And that's exactly how Walt would have wanted it.

Getting Ready to Go

Planning a vacation to Walt Disney World is lots of fun. But it's not as easy as it sounds. There are so many choices to make! Which parks should you visit? What should you pack? And where can you meet your favorite Disney characters? Use this book to answer these questions and help plan your family's vacation. Remember: It's never too early to get started!

Make a Simple Schedule

Did you know that there are more than 300 attractions at Walt Disney World? It could take weeks to see them all. And most people don't have weeks to spend on vacation. That's why it's important to make a schedule before you leave home. Without it, you might miss some of the rides you want to try the most.

What You'll Need
• Paper   • Pencil   • This book

What to Do

1. Write "Magic Kingdom" at the top of a piece of paper.

2. Look at the Magic Kingdom chapter. Every time you see an attraction that sounds like fun, write its name on the paper.

3. When you have finished the chapter, look over your list. Then put a star next to your favorite attractions. These are your "must-sees."

4. Now make a schedule for each of the other theme parks you plan to visit.

5. Don't forget to take your Simple Schedules to the parks!

Learn the Disney Lingo

Audio-Animatronics — Life-like robots, from birds and dinosaurs to movie stars and presidents. They seem real — but they're not.

Cast Member — A Disney worker.

Circle-Vision 360 — A movie that surrounds you. The screens form a circle.

Guidemap — A theme park map that also describes attractions, shops, restaurants, and entertainment.

Imagineer — A creative person who designs Disney shows and attractions.

MagicBand — A wrist band that can serve as a park ticket.

Save Room for Souvenirs

When you pack for your trip, make sure you're prepared for the weather. Believe it or not, it gets chilly in Florida, especially in the winter. But during the summer it's sizzling hot! It's usually warm during the rest of the year. Layers are a good idea, so you can take something off if you get hot. Remember to pack clothes and shoes that are lightweight and comfortable — since you'll do a lot of walking at the parks. And don't overstuff your suitcase. You may need room for the goodies you get at Walt Disney World.

What else should you bring? That's up to you! Here's a short list to help you get started:

- **A sweatshirt or sweater**
- **Comfy sneakers or shoes**
- **Shorts and pants**
- **Long-sleeved and short-sleeved shirts**
- **A hat and sunglasses**
- **A bathing suit**
- **Pajamas**
- **Sunscreen**
- **Bug spray**

Visit Disney on the Internet

This book is filled with information, but there is another great way to learn about Walt Disney World: the Internet. With a parent's permission you can use the *My Disney Experience* mobile app or website, or pay a visit to *www.disneyworld.com*.

If you have a question and don't have access to the Internet, write to:

Walt Disney World
P.O. Box 10000
Lake Buena Vista, FL 32830

COUNTDOWN
TO WALT DISNEY WORLD

10 DAYS TO GO!

Start to plan a Disney dinner party. Select some of your favorite vacation foods for the menu. Who is on your guest list?

_____

_____

_____

9 DAYS TILL DISNEY

Get to work on your Magic Kingdom Simple Schedule. (Read page 12 to learn how.)

Which ride are you going to go on first?

_____

6 DAYS . . .

Make some Mouse ears — tape strips of paper together to make a loop big enough to fit around your head. Then cut out two circles and tape them to the front of the loop. Make a pair for everyone invited to your party.

5 MORE DAYS

Plan your Disney's Hollywood Studios Simple Schedule. The first two should be almost done by now.

And start packing! (Flip to page 13 for some packing tips.)

2 DAYS - JUST 2!

It's party time! Set the table to look festive for your special Disney dinner party. After dessert, share your theme park schedules with your family. Remember to wear your Mouse ears!

1 DAY LEFT - YIPPEE!

Don't stay up too late — tomorrow is the **BIG DAY!**

Take a look at a calendar. On which day does your Walt Disney World vacation begin? Once you find it, count back 10 days — that's the day you can start this special countdown.

To do it, simply color in the number for each day as it arrives. Then try the daily activity. Be sure to ask a grown-up for help. You can make up your own special activities, too!

8 DAYS LEFT

Make a list with addresses of anyone you want to send a postcard to. (Don't forget about e-mail addresses for Internet postcards, too.)

7 DAYS AND COUNTING

It's time to start your Epcot Simple Schedule. Have you finished making your Magic Kingdom schedule yet?

Which attraction do you think sounds best?

_____

4 DAYS NOW!

Pop some popcorn and watch your favorite Disney movie with your family.

Which flick did you pick?

_____

3 DAYS - IT'LL BE SOON!

Spend some time on your Animal Kingdom Simple Schedule tonight. Finish up schedules for the other parks, too. Which theme park are you hoping to visit first? _____

TODAY'S THE DAY!

MONTH / DAY / YEAR

Magic Kingdom

READER
**Favorite
Theme
Park**
PLEASER

PHOTO BY JILL SAFRO

When most people hear the words "Walt Disney World," they think of Cinderella Castle, Splash Mountain, and, of course, Mickey Mouse. They are all here in the Magic Kingdom, along with much more. That's why so many kids say the Magic Kingdom is the most special part of the World.

You can spend lots of time in its six lands — Main Street, U.S.A., Adventureland, Frontierland, Liberty Square, Fantasyland, and Tomorrowland. This chapter will help you decide which attractions you want to see first. Then flip back to page 12. It has tips on how to make a simple Magic Kingdom schedule. That way you can organize your park visit and avoid wasting valuable time.

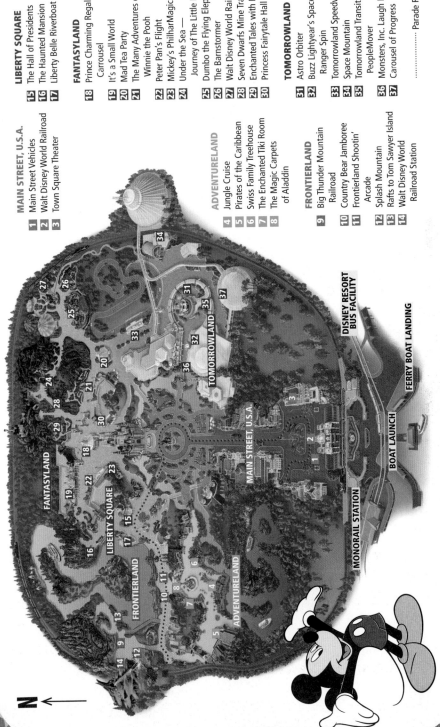

MAIN STREET, U.S.A.
1 Main Street Vehicles
2 Walt Disney World Railroad
3 Town Square Theater

ADVENTURELAND
4 Jungle Cruise
5 Pirates of the Caribbean
6 Swiss Family Treehouse
7 The Enchanted Tiki Room
8 The Magic Carpets
   of Aladdin

FRONTIERLAND
9 Big Thunder Mountain
   Railroad
10 Country Bear Jamboree
11 Frontierland Shootin'
   Arcade
12 Splash Mountain
13 Rafts to Tom Sawyer Island
14 Walt Disney World
   Railroad Station

LIBERTY SQUARE
15 The Hall of Presidents
16 The Haunted Mansion
17 Liberty Belle Riverboat

FANTASYLAND
18 Prince Charming Regal
   Carrousel
19 It's a Small World
20 Mad Tea Party
21 The Many Adventures of
   Winnie the Pooh
22 Peter Pan's Flight
23 Mickey's PhilharMagic
24 Under the Sea —
   Journey of The Little Mermaid
25 Dumbo the Flying Elephant
26 The Barnstormer
27 Walt Disney World Railroad
28 Seven Dwarfs Mine Train
29 Enchanted Tales with Belle
30 Princess Fairytale Hall

TOMORROWLAND
31 Astro Orbiter
32 Buzz Lightyear's Space
   Ranger Spin
33 Tomorrowland Speedway
34 Space Mountain
35 Tomorrowland Transit Authority
   PeopleMover
36 Monsters, Inc. Laugh Floor
37 Carousel of Progress
·············· Parade Route

You can get another map of the Magic Kingdom at the park. It's free!

17

Main Street, U.S.A.

Are you ready for some time traveling? You will do a lot of it in the Magic Kingdom. Four out of its six lands send you either back or forward in time.

Main Street, U.S.A., is one of those lands. It was made to look like a small American town in the year 1900. (Some of it is based on the town Walt Disney grew up in — Marceline, Missouri.)

There are pretty lamp posts, horse-drawn trolleys, and many other touches that make the street charming. If you look both ways before crossing, you'll notice a big difference between this Main Street and a real one: There's a castle at the end of it!

There are no major attractions here, but Main Street is a fun place to be. You can sink your teeth into a fresh-baked cupcake, hop aboard a train, or watch a parade pass by.

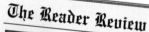

READER TIP

"You can enter Main Street, U.S.A., before the rest of the park opens for the day!"

Christina (age 10)
Los Angeles, CA

The Reader Review

By: Emma, age 12
Deerfield, IL

There's no better cure for sore feet than a trip on the Walt Disney World Railroad. A friendly voice provides information about the park, and there is a nice breeze. It's great for all ages.

Walt Disney World Railroad

Walt Disney loved trains. He even had a miniature one in his backyard that was big enough for him to ride on.

The Magic Kingdom trains are real locomotives that were built nearly a hundred years ago. A full trip takes about 20 minutes, but you can get on or off at any train station (Main Street, U.S.A., Frontierland, or Fantasyland).

What do most kids think about the Magic Kingdom's railroad? They love traveling by train. You get a great view of the park — plus a chance to rest your feet.

HOT TIP!

Town Square Theater is a great place to meet Mickey Mouse. You can even get a Fastpass and skip the long line. Bring your camera!

Main Street Vehicles

The Walt Disney World Railroad isn't the only transportation on Main Street, U.S.A. Horse-drawn trolleys, old-fashioned cars, and an antique fire engine make trips up and down the street early in the day.

You can climb aboard any one of these vehicles in Town Square or by Cinderella Castle. Each trip is strictly one-way — you will be asked to hop off after the ride.

The vehicles do not run every day. Stop by City Hall (it's on Main Street) to find out the schedule.

When the horses that pull the trolleys take a break, they can usually be found in the Car Barn. It's near the Emporium shop on Main Street. Stop by to say hello!

HIDDEN MICKEY ALERT!

Look by the railing around the statue of Walt Disney and Mickey Mouse at the end of Main Street — it casts a Mickey shadow!

PHOTO BY JILL SAFRO

Magic Kingdom

Adventureland

A trip to Adventureland is like a visit to a tropical jungle. It has so many plants and trees that Tarzan would feel right at home. (Don't bother looking for him. He prefers his own treehouse to the one here. It's in Disneyland in California.)

As you can tell from the name of this land, the attractions take you on exciting (and silly) adventures.

HIDDEN MICKEY ALERT!
As you enter Adventureland, look at the shields above the bridge. One has a Hidden Mickey carved into it.

PHOTO BY JILL SAFRO

Jungle Cruise

It's a good thing elephants aren't shy. Otherwise, they might get upset when you watch them take a bath. That's just one of the interesting sights on the Jungle Cruise.

The voyage goes through the jungles of Africa and Asia. Along the way you see life-like zebras, giraffes, lions, hippos, and a few headhunters. (Don't worry — the only real animals in the ride are the human beings inside the boat!)

The Jungle Cruise is usually very crowded — try to get there early in the morning. It's a good idea to ride during the day, when you can see everything. But if you want a spookier ride, take the cruise at night.

The Reader Review

A Great Big Beautiful Day!

By: Shawn, age 12
York, PA

I like this ride because of all the corny jokes the captain tells. They're so funny! I liked the animals better when I was younger, but I still ride to hear those famous jokes!

HIDDEN MICKEY ALERT!
Keep an eye out for the bathing elephants — a Mickey is carved into the rock behind them.

HOT TIP!

Do you think you'd make a good pirate? Find out by joining a quest called A Pirate's Adventure — Treasure of the Seven Seas. You will use a map and a magic charm to help find treasure and keep pirate enemies away!

LOUD
Attraction Reaction

SCARY
Attraction Reaction

DARK
Attraction Reaction

Pirates of the Caribbean

Dead men tell no tales! That's the warning a pirate gives near the start of this attraction. Don't worry — this classic ride isn't going to hurt you. But there is a small dip and some dark scenes, so be prepared.

The journey takes place in a little boat. After floating through a cave... *BOOM!* You're in the middle of a pirate attack! Cannons blast while the song "Yo Ho, Yo Ho, a Pirate's Life for Me" plays in the background.

The pirates and animals look real. But they are Audio-Animatronics figures (kind of like robots). Look for a pirate with his leg hanging over a bridge — the leg is really hairy.

In case you didn't know: This is the attraction that inspired Disney's Pirates of the Caribbean movies. Arrrrrrr!

The Reader Review

A Great Big Beautiful Day!

By: Conor, age 10
Cork, Ireland

My favorite part of the ride is the lady chasing the pirates with a broom! My 6-year-old brother was afraid of the pirate battle. It's really not that scary, but it might be better for older kids.

HOT TIP!

Some riders can control how high or low the carpet flies. If you want this job, ask to sit in the front row of the carpet.

The Reader Review

A Great Big Beautiful Day!

By: Jaiden, age 10
Oregon, WI

I like the Magic Carpets of Aladdin. The ride gives you a great view of Adventureland. And you can cool off when the big camel spits at you!

PHOTO BY JILL SAFRO

The Magic Carpets of Aladdin

If a genie granted you some wishes, what would they be? To be a prince and win the heart of a princess? Well, that was Aladdin's wish, and thanks to his funny friend, Genie, his request came true (eventually).

You won't find a real genie at this ride, but you will get to take a high-flying trip on a magic carpet — much like Aladdin and Jasmine did in the animated movie.

The magic touch

Like Dumbo the Flying Elephant in Fantasyland, riders on The Magic Carpets of Aladdin use gears to control their own carpet's flight.

Also like Dumbo, these magic carpets really soar. Beware of the golden camel — he likes to spit at Magic Kingdom guests!

A whole new world

Kids who visit Adventureland may notice that this area has a special look. The different shops and decorations make it look like the busy marketplace of Agrabah from *Aladdin*. You might even see the characters from the movie during your visit. So keep a pen handy for autographs — Aladdin and Jasmine will be happy to sign them. They'll pose for photos, too.

Swiss Family Treehouse

Before he wrote a book called *The Swiss Family Robinson*, Johann Wyss and his kids imagined what it would be like for their family to be stranded on an island. Together they came up with lots of crazy adventures for the Robinsons. They survive a shipwreck, fight off pirates, and build the most awesome treehouse in the world.

Walt Disney Productions made a movie based on the book in 1960. The Swiss Family Treehouse in Adventureland looks just like the treehouse in the film. In it, you climb a staircase to many different levels. Each room has lots to see. The tree itself looks very real, but it's not. It has 300,000 plastic leaves, and concrete roots.

PHOTO BY MIKE CARROLL

Sorcerers of the Magic Kingdom

Disney villains are trying to take over the Magic Kingdom — and you can help defeat them. How? First, Merlin the magician will make you an apprentice sorcerer. Then you can use magic spell cards to beat the bad guys and save the park!

To play the game, stop at the Firehouse on Main Street and show your MagicBand or park ticket. You will receive everything needed for 9 magical quests: a set of cards, Merlin's mystical map, and a bit of training. (It does not cost extra to play.) As you follow clues, you will try to stop villains from stealing Merlin's crystal ball. Good luck!

Each day you visit the park, you can get new cards at the Firehouse and play again. Spell cards are yours to keep. Many kids enjoy collecting and trading the cards. And spell cards don't expire — you can use them over and over again.

READER TIP

"If you like to collect Sorcerers cards, you may find kids willing to trade with you at the portals in the park." (Make sure you have a grown-up with you when you trade cards.)

Kevin (age 8)
Crystal Lake, IL

23

Walt Disney's Enchanted Tiki Room

PHOTO BY MIKE CARROLL

Birds rule at this attraction. They also sing and crack lots of jokes. If you've been here before, you may know José, Michael, Fritz, and Pierre. They've been singing old favorites like "The Tiki, Tiki, Tiki Room" for nearly 50 years.

So what makes this tiki room enchanted? We already know that the birds all sing — but so do the flowers! In fact, even the masks on the wall get in on the act. The show takes place all around you, so don't forget to look up and behind you. And don't worry — there isn't a bad seat in the house. Be sure to warm up your vocal cords before heading to the Tiki Room — the audience is asked to join in and "sing like the birdies sing." Very small kids may be a little spooked by a thunderstorm.

PHOTO BY MIKE CARROLL

HIDDEN MICKEY ALERT!
Look for a Mickey or two on the bird perches inside the Tiki Room.

Who am I?

- I can't swim
- I ate a rock.
- I'm a chicken.

Answer: Heihei!

Frontierland

Howdy, pardners! And welcome to the Wild West. Frontierland shows you what America was like when pioneers first settled west of the Mississippi River. It's also where you'll find two of the best rides in the Magic Kingdom. Both of them are special Disney mountains. You can take a watery trip down Splash Mountain and ride a runaway train at Big Thunder Mountain Railroad. These are just a few of the fun things to do here.

The Reader Review

By: Dan, age 12
Hummelstown, PA

I think every kid who comes to the Magic Kingdom should explore Tom Sawyer Island. I would have spent more time there if I could. The caves are the best part.

Tom Sawyer Island

There's only one way to get to Tom Sawyer Island — by raft. That's the way Tom himself used to travel. (Tom Sawyer is a character created by the author Mark Twain.)

Don't expect to find any rides here. In fact, compared to the rest of the Magic Kingdom, it's a pretty calm place. But if you bring your imagination, you can have exciting adventures of your own.

Bouncy bridges and secret exits

The island has a real windmill to wander through, hills to climb, and two bridges. One of them is an old barrel bridge. When one person bounces on the bridge, everyone does. (Hold on to the ropes if you are worried about falling.)

Across one bridge is a big fort. An Audio-Animatronics blacksmith is working inside it. And there's a secret exit that is really a path through a dark and narrow cave.

In all, there are three caves to explore. They are the best things on the island. Beware: The caves are quite dark and may be a little scary.

Kids love it here

All of Tom Sawyer Island is popular with younger kids. Some kids think the bridges and caves are the best part.

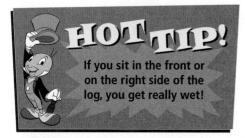

HOT TIP!

If you sit in the front or on the right side of the log, you get really wet!

HIDDEN MICKEY ALERT!

Look in the clouds during the final riverboat scene for a sleeping Mickey. (It comes after the big splash.)

PHOTO BY JILL SAFRO

Splash Mountain

After riding Splash Mountain, you'll know how it got its name. It's impossible to stay dry. There are three small dips leading up to a big, splashy drop into the briar patch.

You're all wet

No matter which seat you sit in, there's a good chance you'll get wet. But if you sit in the front, you're sure to get soaked. Don't worry, you'll dry off fast in the Florida sun.

The scenery tells the story

You travel through scenes from Walt Disney's movie *Song of the South*. You may have to go on it a few times to understand the ride's story.

In it, a character named Br'er Rabbit is trying to get away from Br'er Fox and Br'er Bear. When the rabbit goes over the edge toward the end, you go along for the ride. (Try to keep your eyes open during the big drop — it won't be easy.)

You must be at least 40 inches tall to ride Splash Mountain.

HIDDEN MICKEY ALERT!
This Hidden Mickey is a prickly one —
it's part of a cactus at Big Thunder's exit.

PHOTO BY JILL SAFRO

READER TIP

"During a parade is a good time to go to the most popular attractions — their lines may be shorter than usual."

Joe (age 13)
Roanoke, VA

WILD
Attraction Reaction

FP+

Big Thunder Mountain Railroad

#1 RIDE READER PLEASER

Hang on to your hat and glasses, because this is one of the wildest rides in the wilderness. The speedy trains zip in, out, and over a huge, rocky mountain. They pass through scenes with real-looking chickens, goats, donkeys, and more.

The swoops and turns make this a thrilling roller coaster, but it's a bit tamer than Space Mountain. It's a ride you can go on again and again and see new things each time. Look for funny sights in the town — like the poor guy floating around in a bathtub. Try to ride during the day and again at night.

You must be at least 40 inches tall to ride Big Thunder Mountain.

The Reader Review

A Great Big Beautiful Day!

By: Taylor, age 11
Wyoming, MI

Big Thunder Mountain is a blast! I really like this attraction because it doesn't have a lot of dips. I think older kids would like it best — the hard turns might shock younger ones. What makes this ride seem very scary is the hard stop it comes to at the end.

Country Bear Jamboree

You have probably never seen bears quite like these. They sing songs, play instruments, and tell jokes. This is a silly show, so go in with a silly attitude. Big Al is one of the most popular bears. And he can't even carry a tune!

Everyone gets in on the act

Sometimes the audience sings and claps along with the performers. Even the furry heads on the wall join in on the fun. Melvin the moose, Buff the buffalo, and Buck the deer love to hang around the theater.

What do kids think of the bears?

The kooky country music show gets mixed reviews from kids. Some love it. Others aren't so thrilled. But almost everyone agrees that younger kids seem to enjoy it the most. It's also a great place to cool off and rest up on a hot day.

The Reader Review

By: Matthew, age 11
Peachtree City, GA

Country Bear Jamboree is not that interesting to me because I am not that into country music. I wish it had more talking and less singing. I like that the show is funny. The bears tell some pretty silly jokes!

The Muppets Present . . . Great Moments in American History

Hear ye, hear ye! Liberty Square has some funny, fuzzy friends on hand to tell tales about history: The Muppets. They act and sing in an all-American celebration. It's Muppet-ational!

Have you ever heard about the signing of the U.S. Declaration of Independence? Or Paul Revere's famous ride? Now's your chance. The Muppets — Kermit the Frog, Miss Piggy, Fozzie Bear, The Great Gonzo, and Sam Eagle — bring these stories to life in the windows above Liberty Square. There are no seats, but everybody gets a pretty good view of the action. Most kids enjoy the funny, patriotic performances. Check a Times Guide for showtimes on the day you visit the Magic Kingdom.

Liberty Square

What did America look like in Colonial days? Parts of it looked like Liberty Square. This small area separates Frontierland from Fantasyland. It's a quiet spot with some shops and a couple of popular attractions.

The Haunted Mansion

This haunted house isn't too scary, but there are plenty of ghosts to keep you on your toes. Before you enter, enjoy the interactive wait area and read the funny tombstones outside. (We like the one that says: HERE LIES GOOD OLD FRED. A GREAT BIG ROCK FELL ON HIS HEAD.)

Once inside, you'll be stranded in a room with no windows and no doors. For a while, it seems like there's no way out. It is spooky!

There's a moment before you board a "Doom Buggy" when the room is totally dark. It's just a few seconds, but for some, it's too long.

The Doom Buggy doesn't move very fast, but it is still hard to catch all the details. Watch for the door knockers that knock all by themselves, a ghostly teapot pouring tea, and a ghost napping under the table at a party in the ballroom.

The Reader Review

A Great Big Beautiful Day!

By: Will, age 12
Greenville, SC

The Haunted Mansion is spooky at first, but then it is loads of fun. My favorite scene is the waltzing ghosts. Older kids will enjoy this attraction. Younger kids might find this scary. I think it's a *very* cool ride.

The Hall of Presidents

The first part of this attraction is a film about U.S. history. Then the screen rises and all of the American presidents are on stage together. They are robots called Audio-Animatronics, but they look real.

If you watch closely, you'll notice the presidents move, nod, and blink.

The attraction is inside a building that looks like Independence Hall. (The real Independence Hall is in Philadelphia, Pennsylvania.) Each show is about 22 minutes long.

The Reader Review

By: Amy, age 11
Toms River, NJ

It's amazing how real the presidents look. Kids interested in history will really enjoy the show, but others might find it too long.

Liberty Belle Riverboat

The *Liberty Belle* riverboat docks in Liberty Square. This big steamboat takes guests on slow, relaxing cruises. It can be a nice break on a busy day (though there aren't many seats). The best spots are right up front or in the back, where you can see both sides of the river as you float along. The 47-foot-tall boat uses steam fuel. The steam powers the paddle wheel, which makes the boat move. Pretty cool!

Fantasyland

Fantasyland is home to many magical rides that younger kids love. Older kids and even grown-ups enjoy them, too. These attractions are very popular, and the waits can be quite long. But the lines are sometimes a bit shorter while people watch an afternoon parade or join in a dance party. It's a good idea to skip the parade one day and spend time in Fantasyland. The land may be less crowded late in the day, too.

Prince Charming Regal Carrousel

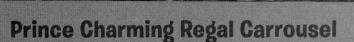

Just about all of the attractions at Walt Disney World were dreamed up by Disney Imagineers. But not this carrousel. It was discovered in New Jersey, where it was once part of another amusement park. It was built around 1917.

When you climb on a horse for your ride on the carrousel, be sure to notice that each horse is different. And remember to look up at the ceiling and its hand-painted scenes from *Cinderella*. While you ride, listen for famous Disney tunes, including "When You Wish Upon a Star" and "Be Our Guest."

READER TIP

"If you want to meet Cinderella, have a meal at Cinderella's Royal Table in the castle. She'll be in the lobby!" (You can also meet her in Fantasyland at Princess Fairytale Hall.)

Christine (age 10)
Horsham, PA

Mad Tea Party

The idea for the giant teacups that spin through this ride came from a famous scene in *Alice in Wonderland*. In the movie, the Mad Hatter throws himself a tea party to celebrate his un-birthday. That's any day of the year that is not his birthday!

On the Mad Tea Party ride, you control how fast your cup spins by turning the big wheel in the center. The more you turn, the more you spin. Or you can just sit back and let the cup spin on its own. It may be hard while you're whirling, but try to take a peek at the little mouse that keeps popping out of the big teapot in the center. He's cute.

The Reader Review

By: Elizabeth, age 11
Jackson, GA

This ride is fun for the whole family. It's best when everyone helps spin. But if you get dizzy easily, don't turn the wheel, and try not to look outside of your cup as it spins!

The Barnstormer

One of the wildest rides in Fantasyland is a roller coaster in Storybook Circus. This ride may look small, but it packs plenty of thrills. It takes you on a twisting and turning flight high above the park.

The trip starts out slow, but watch out! Before you know it, you will be swooping and soaring through the circus. Hang on tight!

Before you board, be sure to check out the magical area surrounding the ride — that Goofy really is quite goofy. You must be at least 35 inches tall to ride this mini roller coaster.

The Reader Review

By: Samantha, age 8
Chicago, IL

Even though this ride is short, it is awesome! I love it when you fly through the Goofy sign. I always get a Fastpass for this wild ride.

Dumbo the Flying Elephant

Just like the star of the movie *Dumbo*, these elephants know how to fly. They would love to take you for a short ride (about two minutes) above Fantasyland. A button lets you control the up-and-down movement of the elephant.

Take your kid brother or sister

Many kids agree that this ride is the most fun for younger kids, from age 3 to 10. But they all find something to like and think it would be fun to go on with a younger brother or sister.

Beware of long lines

Even though Dumbo has doubled in size (so more people can ride), the line for this attraction tends to be long. Get a Fastpass if you can. If not, you can play in the circus playground area while you wait. (A special pager will tell you when it is your turn to ride Dumbo.) If the wait is too long when you get there, try again toward the end of the day. That's when many young kids have already gone home.

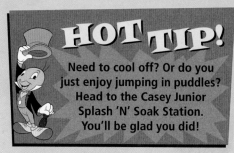

HOT TIP!

Need to cool off? Or do you just enjoy jumping in puddles? Head to the Casey Junior Splash 'N' Soak Station. You'll be glad you did!

The Reader Review

A Great Big Beautiful Day!

By: Rachel, age 10
Franklin, TN

I think this ride is more fun if you go on it with your little brother or sister. I like that you can control how high or low you want to be.

HOT TIP!

Would you like to meet Disney princesses? Head to Princess Fairytale Hall! Royal folks such as Cinderella and Rapunzel greet guests throughout the day.

#13 RIDE PLEASER

READER PLEASER

Peter Pan's Flight

DARK Attraction Reaction

FP+

Swoop and soar through scenes that tell the story of how Wendy, Michael, and John get sprinkled with pixie dust and fly off to Never Land with Peter Pan and Tinker Bell. Along the way, you see Princess Tiger Lily, Captain Hook, and Hook's sidekick, Mr. Smee.

Near the beginning of the trip, there's a beautiful scene of London at night. Notice that the cars on the streets really move. Later, watch out for the crocodile that wants to munch on Captain Hook.

When you first board your pirate ship, it seems like you're riding on a track on the ground. Once you get going, the track is actually above you, so it feels like the ship is really flying.

The Reader Review

A Great Big Beautiful Day!

By: Lila, age 12
Cape Elizabeth, ME

Peter Pan's flight is one of my all-time favorite rides at Disney World. I love how you fly over London and join Peter and his friends on their magical adventure. This attraction is fun, no matter what your age.

READER #14 RIDE PLEASER

It's a Small World

People have a lot in common, no matter where they live. That's the point of this attraction. In it, you take a slow boat ride through several large rooms where singing dolls represent different parts of the world. There are Greek dancers, Japanese kite flyers, Scottish bagpipers, and many more. There's also a jungle scene with hippos, giraffes, and monkeys.

All this colorful scenery is set to the song "It's a Small World, After All."

The signs at the end say good-bye in different languages. *Aloha! Shalom! Sayonara! Adios!*

The Reader Review

A Great Big Beautiful Day!

By: Maggie, age 11
Lee's Summit, MO

Nobody should pass up this classic attraction! I love seeing all the different cultures and guessing where the dolls come from. All ages will enjoy It's a Small World.

FP+

READER TIP

"Book Fastpass as early as you can. They might be all given away quickly!"

Christopher (age 11)
Valley View, OH

The Many Adventures of Winnie the Pooh

Winnie the Pooh loves his honey. In fact, he'll do anything to keep the sweet treat safe. On this trip through the Hundred Acre Wood, see what Pooh must do to rescue his honey pots and his friends, too.

The blustery day

The wind is howling, the leaves are rustling, and everything in Pooh's world is blowing away. Roo and Piglet are up in the air. And Owl's house is about to topple over. Hold on tight, or you just might be swept away next!

A sticky situation

Finally the wind calms and Pooh can get to sleep. But when he wakes up from his silly dream, it's raining outside. Pooh's honey pots are about to wash away. He can save them, but will he save himself? Keep in mind that some kids think the interactive wait area is as much fun as the attraction itself. Be sure to check it out!

The Reader Review

By: Ryan, age 11
Milford, MA

My family and I love this ride. My favorite part is when you bounce like Tigger. Get a Fastpass because the line can get very long. You don't want to be saying, "Oh, bother."

Under the Sea — Journey of The Little Mermaid

This attraction invites you to join Ariel for a colorful adventure. Are you ready to dive in? You'll go "under the sea" by boarding a special vehicle called a clam-mobile. (They are giant shells, like the ones over at The Seas with Nemo and Friends in Epcot.) And don't worry about getting wet — the water here is just a cool special effect.

Once you board your clam-mobile, the journey begins. Along the way, you will meet up with Ariel, Flounder, and all of their pals. There is a lot to see and hear in this attraction — you may have to ride it twice to take it all in!

PHOTO BY JILL SAFRO

Seven Dwarfs Mine Train

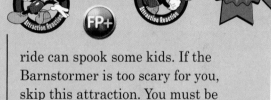

Are you ready to journey into the mine where a million diamonds shine? Then head to the Seven Dwarfs Mine Train! The popular attraction is a roller coaster with a twist — the cars move up and down along the track and they sway a bit from side to side!

Heigh ho, heigh ho!

If you have seen Disney's *Snow White and the Seven Dwarfs*, you know where Sleepy, Dopey, Doc, and their friends work — in a diamond mine. At this attraction, guests board train cars and visit that colorful mine.

Hang on tight

It's not as speedy as Space Mountain, or as rough as the big drop in Splash Mountain, but this ride can spook some kids. If the Barnstormer is too scary for you, skip this attraction. You must be at least 38 inches tall to ride.

The Reader Review

By: Gianna, age 10
Au Gres, MI

If you are looking for a fun ride, stop here! I love the sharp turns and the big drop. Make sure to see the dwarfs and the gems in the mine. I think this is a great ride for people of all ages. You should go at least twice!

Mickey's PhilharMagic

It's magical. It's musical. It's three-dimensional. It's Mickey's PhilharMagic.

Donald Duck is the real star of this 3-D movie, but it's not a one-duck show. He is joined by characters such as Ariel, Aladdin, Jasmine, Simba, and, of course, Mickey Mouse.

A one and a two and a three-D

The show takes place in a grand concert hall. Once guests (that's you!) find seats and put on special 3-D glasses, it's showtime.

Sit back, relax, and enjoy as the cast of characters show off their musical talents. (Some are more talented than others.) And be sure to keep your eyes and ears open — a whole lot happens at the same time.

Eye-popping 3-D effects take place on the oversize screen. Music fills the air. And special surprises happen inside the theater.

What's a PhilharMagic?

In case you were wondering . . . Walt Disney World made up the word PhilharMagic. It's based on the real word *philharmonic*, which describes a bunch of musicians who all play their instruments at the same time.

The Reader Review

By: Megan, age 9
Quincy, IL

Wow! Aladdin and Jasmine fly over your head in this amazing attraction. Lots of other characters pop off the screen, too. Put this on your list of shows to see!

Enchanted Tales with Belle

Would you like to help Belle tell "the tale as old as time" — the story of Beauty and the Beast? You are invited to her dad's cottage to do just that. The experience starts by taking a step through a big, magical mirror.

It transports guests all the way to Beast's castle. There you will meet Madame Wardrobe and her assistant. Together they will assign roles to audience members — be sure to wave your hand when they ask for volunteers. Once all the roles are assigned, guests walk to the library. Expect to be greeted by Lumiere, the friendly candlestick from *Beauty and the Beast*. When Belle arrives, it's story time. This is a popular attraction, and the long line moves slowly. Get a Fastpass if you can.

The Reader Review

By: Emma, age 8
Pleasant Grove, UT

I like Enchanted Tales with Belle. I got to play a part and help act out the story. I think older kids and younger kids will like it a lot. Plus, you get your picture taken with Belle!

Tomorrowland

Tomorrowland began as a view of the future. But as the real world changed, so did this land. Now it's like a city from a science-fiction story. The palm trees are made of metal. The rides here let you rocket through space or zoom through the Magic Kingdom sky. And a famous Space Ranger pops in to visit with guests. A good way to see this land is to ride on the Tomorrowland Transit Authority PeopleMover — it's a relaxing tour and a nice way to give your feet a rest. And even though you won't have a driver's license until the future, you can drive a car in Tomorrowland (as long as you are at least 54 inches tall).

Tomorrowland Transit Authority PeopleMover

This slow-moving ride travels by or through many Tomorrowland attractions. You will even get a peek at Buzz Lightyear's Space Ranger Spin. But pay attention, because you pass by the window very quickly. You'll also go through Space Mountain, but you won't see much because it's totally dark.

This ride is a good one to head to when it's hot out. The cars move just fast enough to create a nice breeze.

It's interesting to know that the ride doesn't make any pollution. And the wait is usually very short.

The Reader Review

By: Sydney, age 10
Leland, NC

I love the thrill of riding around Tomorrowland and going through attractions. The turns can be a bit bumpy, but the ride is mostly relaxing. My dad and I love to look for Hidden Mickeys.

Space Mountain

Thrill seekers head straight for this rocket ride through outer space. It has twists, turns, and a few steep dips. And it all takes place in the dark! Space Mountain is one of the most popular rides in Walt Disney World.

#4 RIDE PLEASER

Who turned out the lights?

It's so dark inside Space Mountain that you barely see where you are going — especially if you sit in the front of the rocket. That's what makes the ride so exciting. Every curve comes as a surprise.

You will hear sounds of other rockets zooming by. But don't worry. The coaster is perfectly safe. The noises are meant to add to the excitement.

Is it too scary?

There's no doubt about it: Space Mountain is scary. But some kids say it's a "good scary." The rockets only travel about 28 miles per hour, but it feels much faster. You must be at least 44 inches tall to ride.

The Reader Review

A Great Big Beautiful Day!

By: Erin, age 12
Barrington, IL

This is one of my all-time favorite rides in Disney World! You are completely in the dark, so you can't see *anything*. You don't know when you are going to turn or drop! Unless you're afraid of the dark (or roller coasters), I recommend Space Mountain.

READER TIP

"For the shortest lines, be there when the park opens!"

Whitney (age 12)
Mount Pleasant, MI

PHOTO BY JILL SAFRO

Walt Disney's Carousel of Progress

A lot has changed since the year 1900. Most homes had no electricity, water came from a well, and nobody had a TV. Life was rough! This attraction shows how American family life has changed since then.

A moving experience

The show is really four short plays. And the performers are all Audio-Animatronics actors. After each scene, the theater moves to the right. That's when you will hear the song "There's a Great, Big, Beautiful Tomorrow." Feel free to sing along.

Walt made it special

Some kids may find the show a bit on the slow side, but others think it's quite special. Why? It was introduced to the world by Walt Disney himself. The special event didn't happen at Disney World (it wasn't open yet), but at the World's Fair in New York City in 1964. Of course, the attraction has been updated (there has been a lot of progress since then), but the show is still an amusing look at American life. And the Carousel of Progress has made history, too — it has had more performances than any other stage show in the history of American theater.

The Reader Review

By: Nicole, age 12
Sunburst, MT

This is a classic show that should not be missed. I recommend this attraction for kids who are interested in history. It teaches you about life from the 1900s to the 1990s.

HIDDEN MICKEY ALERT!

Watch the planets carefully as they whiz by during the short movie. One of them is extra special — it has a Mickey on it!

HOT TIP!

To get more points on the Buzz Lightyear ride, hold the button down the whole time and aim at small, moving, or faraway targets.

#12 RIDE PLEASER

The Reader Review

A Great Big Beautiful Day!

By: Lydia, age 13
Sutton, MA

Everyone will love this ride — it feels like you are in a video game! And you get better at it every time you go on. I think this is the coolest ride in the Magic Kingdom. I recommend getting a Fastpass assignment.

Buzz Lightyear's Space Ranger Spin

FP+

In this attraction, everyone is a toy — including you. In fact, you are so small, you fit inside a video game shooting gallery.

To infinity and beyond!

The ride is under the command of Buzz Lightyear. You've just become a Junior Space Ranger, so you're under his command, too. Together, you battle the evil Emperor Zurg.

Zap that Zurg

Zurg and his robots are stealing batteries from other toys. They plan to use the batteries to power their ultimate weapon of destruction. Your job is to fight back. Use the laser cannons in your spaceship to aim at the targets (they look like Zs) and zap Zurg's power. Every time you hit a target, you earn more points. There is a scoreboard next to the laser cannon. It keeps track of all the points you earn.

At the end of the ride, you'll pass a chart. It shows everyone's ranger rank based on their score. Check to see where your score falls. Most kids improve with practice.

Monsters, Inc. Laugh Floor

PHOTO BY: JILL SAFRO

Buzz Lightyear has some funny neighbors here in Tomorrowland — Mike, Roz, and other kooky characters from the movie *Monsters, Inc.* They are all part of a silly attraction that lets you interact with your animated friends. That's right, the audience members not only watch the show — they are a part of it. Don't worry. The monsters don't want to make kids scream the way they did in the movie. This time, they want to make kids laugh. So be prepared for lots of wackiness and some very silly jokes!

READER TIP

"If you're afraid of heights, skip Astro Orbiter!"

Derek (age 13)
Spokane, WA

Magic Kingdom

Astro Orbiter

In the middle of Tomorrowland, there is a giant, glowing tower. It is called Rocket Tower. The Astro Orbiter ride is all the way at the top. In it, you soar past colorful planets high above Tomorrowland.

Like on Dumbo the Flying Elephant, you control how high or low your rocket flies. You can ride by yourself or with a friend. (Each rocket fits two people.) But if you want to be the one to control how high you go, be sure to sit in the front.

The Reader Review

By: Matthew, age 13
Lakeland, FL

I love going on this ride! Some kids may be scared, but older kids will probably like it best because it goes up very high and tilts when you reach the top.

#15 RIDE *READER PLEASER*

TOMORROWLAND SPEEDWAY

Tomorrowland Speedway

FP+

You don't need a license to drive a car around this racetrack (as long as you're at least 54 inches tall). The race cars travel along a rail, but it's not as easy to drive as it looks. Even experts bounce around a bit — and laugh a lot. The cars are real and are powered by gasoline.

The car does not have a brake pedal. To stop, you just take your foot off the gas pedal.

If you are not tall enough to drive alone, you can still steer the car — just make sure your passenger is at least 54 inches tall. This attraction may not be open in all of 2019.

The Reader Review

A Great Big Beautiful Day!

By: Lauren, age 12
Harrisburg, PA

I love this ride. No matter what your age (if you are at least 54 inches tall), you can drive your parents for once! The race track is nice and long. The line to ride is long, too — but it's worth the wait.

READER TIP

"If you get lost at Walt Disney World, don't worry. Just go to the nearest Cast Member (a worker wearing a name tag) and ask for help."

Sam (age 9)
Eatontown, NJ

Entertainment

The Magic Kingdom is a very entertaining place. It seems like there is always a show starting or a parade going by. Read on to learn about some of the special events that take place in the park. For more information, check a park Times Guide. You can get one at the entrance to the park, at Guest Relations, or in many of the park's shops.

FESTIVAL OF FANTASY PARADE

Disney characters star in this afternoon parade. You might even get to meet characters as they pass by. Say hi to Anna and Elsa on the *Frozen* float! And don't miss the giant fire-breathing dragon. It is super cool. Line up early to get a good spot on the curb.

This parade usually runs during the afternoon. Check a Times Guide for the schedule.

ONCE UPON A TIME

Cinderella Castle becomes a giant movie screen during this 14-minute show. In it, Chip asks Mrs. Potts to tell him a story. She is happy to share tales from *Cinderella*, *Peter Pan*, *Tangled*, *Winnie the Pooh*, *Alice in Wonderland*, and more.

This show happens before the nightly fireworks. Check a Times Guide for the schedule.

CAPTAIN JACK SPARROW'S PIRATE TUTORIAL

Yo, ho, yo, ho! Join Captain Jack and his sidekick, Mac, for this special ceremony — and become a pirate in the process. A few lucky kids get to take part in the show. At the end, everyone takes a pirate oath and sings "Yo Ho — a Pirate's Life for Me." The outdoor show takes place in Adventureland, across from Pirates of the Caribbean.

CASEY'S CORNER PIANO

If you visit Main Street during the day, you'll hear cheery tunes being played on a piano. Some are Disney songs and others are old-fashioned ones that your parents will know. They'll all make you tap your toes. You will find the piano player outside Casey's Corner restaurant on Main Street, U.S.A.

THE MAIN STREET TROLLEY SHOW

If you visit the Magic Kingdom before lunchtime, you may catch this old-fashioned musical show. In it, 12 performers arrive on a very jolly trolley and break into song and dance. You just might find yourself singing or humming along — especially to "Walkin' Right Down the Middle of Main Street, U.S.A." It's a catchy tune!

MOVE IT, SHAKE IT, DANCE AND PLAY IT!

Are you ready to dance?! This rockin' party happens on select days on Main Street, U.S.A. The best part? Disney characters dance along with guests! Expect dancing pals such as Mickey, Minnie, Donald, Chip and Dale, Stitch, and more.

FLAG RETREAT

A special flag ceremony takes place daily. Guests gather around the American flag in Town Square and recite the Pledge of Allegiance. Then the American flag is lowered for the day and a band plays patriotic songs. The Flag Retreat happens in Town Square on Main Street, U.S.A., at about 5 o'clock in the afternoon.

THE ROYAL MAGIC MAKERS

How do young royals learn to be little lords and ladies? By paying close attention to the Royal Majesty Makers — the official experts of Cinderella's court. Sir Sterling, Lady Llewellyn, and their friends teach and entertain folks in the Castle Courtyard in Fantasyland. Listen carefully as Sir Sterling directs you through a game of "Sir Sterling Says." Expect to ride an imaginary horse and slay an invisible dragon. Then you will dance to the sounds of the Royal Majesty Makers band. Shows take place throughout the day. Check a park Times Guide for the schedule.

THE MUPPETS PRESENT . . . GREAT MOMENTS IN AMERICAN HISTORY

The Muppets' take on American history is a little wacky — but it is also quite entertaining. See for yourself at this funny, outdoor show in Liberty Square. It happens in the windows around the Hall of Presidents attraction. Check a Times Guide for the schedule during your visit.

DAPPER DANS

The Dapper Dans are a four-person singing group known as a Barbershop Quartet. They entertain guests on Main Street, U.S.A., throughout the day. Stop in for a show at the barbershop or out on Main Street. They may even perform from their bicycle built for four. That's talent!

MICKEY'S ROYAL FRIENDSHIP FAIRE

Mickey and his pals like to celebrate their friendship with song and dance — and they want you to join them. The musical show takes place in front of Cinderella Castle most days. In it, Disney friends perform to music from *The Princess and the Frog*, *Frozen*, *Tangled*, and other films.

The fun includes appearances by many Disney characters — Goofy, Donald, Daisy, Rapunzel, Flynn Rider, Anna, Elsa, Olaf, Minnie, and Mickey.

Since this show is on an outdoor stage, it may be cancelled if the weather is bad.

HAPPILY EVER AFTER

There is a happy ending to every day at the Magic Kingdom! This fireworks show takes place above and around Cinderella Castle. It captures the heart, humor, and heroism of Disney films.

The show also includes animated projections, laser lights, and merry music. It lasts for about 18 minutes. Don't worry if you can't find space to watch on Main Street — the fireworks can be seen from lots of spots around the park.

The Reader Review

*By: Sarah, age 11
Pinckney, MI*

I love this amazing fireworks show. The special effects make it seem like the characters are right on the castle! Do not miss this "only at Walt Disney World" experience!

MAIN STREET PHILHARMONIC

A marching band makes merry music on Main Street, U.S.A. All of the band members wear bright, red and white uniforms, so they are easy to spot. But there is an easier way to find them: Follow your ears!

Where to find
Characters
at the MAGIC KINGDOM

Characters greet guests all over the park. A great place to meet Mickey Mouse is Main Street's **Town Square Theater**. Tinker Bell is usually there, too. Lots of different characters greet guests on **Main Street** throughout the day.

Looking for Disney princesses? Go to **Princess Fairytale Hall** in Fantasyland. Minnie, Daisy, Goofy, and Donald hang out at **Pete's Silly Sideshow** in the **Storybook Circus** part of Fantasyland. Elsewhere in **Fantasyland** you may find Alice and her Wonderland friends, plus Peter Pan, Gaston, Ariel, Winnie the Pooh, Tigger, and more. Aladdin and Jasmine greet guests in **Adventureland**.

When you're in **Tomorrowland**, keep an eye out for Buzz Lightyear and Stitch.

Merida from *Brave* mingles with park guests in the **Fairytale Garden** (an area next to the Castle).

Another way to see favorite Disney pals is at parades and stage shows. You may get to dance with some of them, too! Check a Magic Kingdom Times Guide for schedules.

Magic Kingdom

Magic Kingdom

Tips

Head to this theme park first, since it has the most rides for kids.

Try to arrive just before the park opens and watch Let the Magic Begin. It's a character-filled show on the stage at Cinderella Castle.

You can meet Mickey Mouse in Main Street's Town Square Theater. Use page 142 of this book for his autograph. Bring a camera, too!

Need a break from long lines? These attractions usually have short waits: The PeopleMover, Country Bear Jamboree, The Enchanted Tiki Room, Carousel of Progress, and The Walt Disney World Railroad.

Need to cool off on a hot day? Get wet at Casey Junior Splash and Soak Station in Fantasyland. Or hop on the PeopleMover and enjoy the breeze.

If the park is open late, it's fun to go on your favorite outdoor attractions after dark.

There are "chicken exits" in the lines for all scary rides, just in case you change your mind about riding at the last minute.

Do not eat just before riding The Barnstormer, Seven Dwarfs Mine Train, Space Mountain, Big Thunder Mountain Railroad, or the Mad Tea Party.

If you've never been on a roller coaster, ride The Barnstormer first. If you enjoy it, try Seven Dwarfs Mine Train — but remember, it is a little scarier!

Bring a big pen for characters to use while signing autographs — big pens are easier to grip.

Attraction Ratings

Magic Kingdom

COOL
(Check It Out)

- Country Bear Jamboree
- Monsters, Inc. Laugh Floor
- Prince Charming Regal Carrousel
- Swiss Family Treehouse
- Liberty Belle Riverboat
- Walt Disney's Enchanted Tiki Room
- Walt Disney's Carousel of Progress
- Walt Disney World Railroad
- The Hall of Presidents

REALLY COOL
(Don't Miss)

- Astro Orbiter
- Mad Tea Party
- Jungle Cruise
- Mickey's PhilharMagic
- Dumbo the Flying Elephant
- Enchanted Tales with Belle
- The Magic Carpets of Aladdin
- The Muppets Present . . . Great Moments in American History
- Tom Sawyer Island
- The Barnstormer
- Under the Sea — Journey of The Little Mermaid
- Tomorrowland Transit Authority PeopleMover

THE COOLEST
(See at least twice)

- Splash Mountain
- Big Thunder Mountain Railroad
- Haunted Mansion
- Peter Pan's Flight
- Buzz Lightyear's Space Ranger Spin
- Pirates of the Caribbean
- The Many Adventures of Winnie the Pooh
- Space Mountain
- It's a Small World
- Seven Dwarfs Mine Train
- Tomorrowland Speedway

What do YOU think?

The kids who helped with this book rated all the attractions at Walt Disney World. But your opinion counts, too! Make your own "Attraction Ratings" list for each park and send it to us. We will use it when we create next year's book. (Our address is on page 7.)

Where's Mickey?

Disney Imagineers have hidden Mickey's image all over the Magic Kingdom. Here are a few places to search for Hidden Mickeys while you are in the park. If you want to meet Mickey in person, go to the Town Square Theater. He's there every day!

The Haunted Mansion

In the ghost party room, check out the bottom of the banquet table. There is a Hidden Mickey made out of two saucers and a plate.

Tomorrowland Transit Authority PeopleMover

After passing the Metro Retro Society, look to the right. There you'll see a lady getting her hair done. What's on her belt? A Hidden Mickey!

Buzz Lightyear's Space Ranger Spin

Once you enter the Buzz building, look for a poster on the right and find the planet called Pollost Prime. One of the continents on the map forms Mickey's profile. And keep your eyes open during the attraction's space video scene (about halfway through). You'll see this same planet fly by on the right.

Carousel of Progress

There are a few Hidden Mickeys in this attraction's Christmas scene. Our favorite is the one on top of the fireplace. It is a Mickey nutcracker! Can you find others?

It's a Small World

During the ride, pay close attention in the Africa room. If you search the purple leaves on the ceiling, you may spot several Hidden Mickeys. (They are close to the giraffes.)

Epcot

Epcot is a great place to make discoveries about the world. At this park, things that used to seem ordinary suddenly become fun. All of the attractions at Epcot are in buildings called pavilions (pronounced: *puh-VILL-yuhnz*). The pavilions are in two sections of the park. One section is Future World, and the other is World Showcase. Future World celebrates inventions and ideas. It shows how they affect everything, from the food you eat and your family car to the land, sea, and outer space. (Some details may change.)

World Showcase lets you travel around the world without leaving the park! There are many different countries to visit here. Each country has copies of its famous buildings, restaurants, and other landmarks. Together, they will make you feel as if you are visiting the real place.

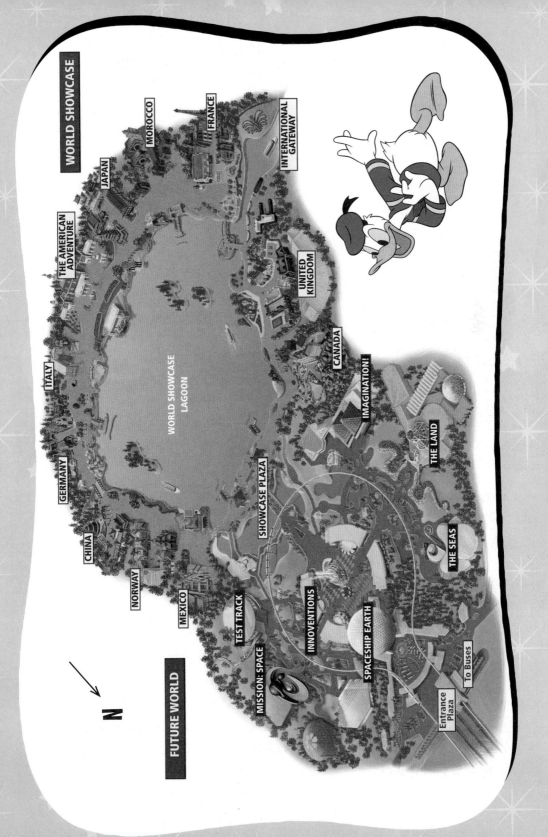

WORLD SHOWCASE

MOROCCO

FRANCE

JAPAN

INTERNATIONAL GATEWAY

THE AMERICAN ADVENTURE

UNITED KINGDOM

ITALY

CANADA

GERMANY

IMAGINATION!

WORLD SHOWCASE LAGOON

THE LAND

CHINA

THE SEAS

NORWAY

SHOWCASE PLAZA

MEXICO

TEST TRACK

INNOVENTIONS

N

MISSION: SPACE

SPACESHIP EARTH

FUTURE WORLD

Entrance Plaza

To Buses

Use this map to explore Epcot.

53

Future World

When you enter Epcot by monorail, you are in the area called Future World. Some of the attractions here are educational — but that doesn't mean you won't have fun. Take it from other kids: There's a lot to discover.

READER TIP

"The line for Spaceship Earth is usually shortest toward the end of the day!"

Kersie (age 12)
Vancouver, WA

Spaceship Earth

  FP+

You can't miss the silver ball that is the symbol of Epcot. It's gigantic! The Spaceship Earth ride is inside this big, round building. (It's called a geosphere.) The attraction explores the ways people have shaped the future throughout history. You'll have a chance to create your own vision of the future. How? By using a touch screen inside your ride vehicle.

The journey takes place in slow-moving time machine vehicles. When the ride is over, you can visit the "Project Tomorrow" area. It's filled with interactive exhibits.

The Reader Review

 A Great Big Beautiful Day!

By: Amy, age 12
Clinton, NJ

Some people think this ride is not worth a long wait, but it's one of my family's favorites. It may be a calm ride, but I think it's very interesting. It's a classic!

Mission: SPACE

PHOTO BY JILL SAFRO

Three . . . two . . . one . . . blast-off! This ride lets you know what it's like to be an astronaut on a trip to outer space. Here, you can take a rocket to Mars or enjoy a trip around Earth.

The Mars voyage is the Orange Mission. It is very intense. The orbit around our planet is much calmer. It's called the Green Mission.

Each spacecraft holds four guests. Once aboard, it's time for take-off. You will feel the tug of gravity during the Orange Mission launch — just like on a NASA spacecraft. This part lasts nearly a minute, so be ready.

What's your job?

Once you're on your way, things calm down a bit. That may be when you realize you have a job to do. Are you the commander, engineer, pilot, or navigator? That depends on where you sit. It doesn't matter — all the jobs are fun to do. Just before the Orange Mission ends, you will get a strange sensation. It's not weightlessness, but it is definitely out of this world. It's a lot like the feeling astronauts get in outer space.

Mission accomplished

If bouncing or spinning makes you sick, skip the Orange Mission — a lot of people get quite woozy on it. Some feel sick afterward. You can take a cool trip around the earth, instead — just ask for the Green Mission. You must be at least 40 inches tall to ride either version. Be sure to check the Advanced Training Lab near the Mission: SPACE exit. It has activities that are out of this world.

Epcot

The Seas with Nemo & Friends

It's easy to find Nemo these days — he is at The Seas pavilion at Epcot! He and his friends can't wait for you to visit. There are more than 2,000 real sea creatures living here. There is also a ride, a shark-themed area, and interesting sea-based exhibits to explore. Details may change in 2019.

The Seas with Nemo & Friends

Jump inside a clam-mobile and let the adventure begin. It's a class trip run by Nemo's teacher, Mr. Ray. It seems little Nemo has wandered off again. Your job is to help find him. Expect to meet up with Dory, Bruce, Chum, Crush, Squirt, and others along the way. And don't worry — Nemo won't stay lost for long.

Hands-on fun

After taking a quick look at the aquarium, you'll enter an area called Sea Base. This is your chance to take a closer look at the creatures and to try out the hands-on exhibits. Be sure to visit the Nemo and Friends room, where you can find a real-life version of the little guy. Many kids get a kick out of Bruce's Shark World. (It's a cool play area where you can learn about sharks.)

The Reader Review

By: Lauren, age 14
Deerfield Beach, FL

My family and I spent hours at this pavilion. The ride is superb and is home to thousands of gorgeous fish. Be sure to check out the manatees. They're adorable!

Turtle Talk with Crush

Everyone seems to love Turtle Talk with Crush. It's a show that lets you talk to the 150-year-old cartoon critter. The best part? He talks back.

The show takes place in a small theater. Grown-ups like to sit on the benches, but most kids prefer to sit on the floor in front of the big screen. From the moment Crush swims onto the big screen, he has everybody laughing. He will ask the audience questions, tell some jokes, and make comments about the different "shells" kids are wearing. He may even talk

to YOU! Dory may stop in for a visit, too. Turtle Talk with Crush lasts about 10 minutes. The show is totally awesome, dude.

The Reader Review

A Great Big Beautiful Day!

By: Carl, age 9
Kenton, OH

Turtle Talk is neat because you can tell Crush things and he answers back. It was really fun. I wish Crush could live at my house.

Bruce's Sub House

Finding Nemo's Bruce the shark has a special play zone in The Seas pavilion. The Sub House has a small maze and a very large version of Bruce himself. It is so big, kids and their families can fit inside! This is a great place to take a picture, so have your camera ready. Bruce's friends Anchor and Chum are on hand for photos, too. Older kids enjoy reading all about sharks and playing video games about the mighty sea creatures.

The Land

PHOTO BY JILL SAFRO

The building called The Land looks like a big greenhouse. One of its attractions focuses on food and where it comes from. It's a boat ride called Living with the Land. The other attraction is a high-flying hang-glider ride known as Soarin' Around the World. Most kids love it. (Most grown-ups do, too!)

HIDDEN MICKEY ALERT!
Study the paintings while you wait in line for Living with the Land. One has bubbles on it that connect to form a Mickey head.

Living with the Land

 FP+

What's the most popular fruit on our planet? The banana! People eat more bananas than any other fruity snack. You'll learn lots more food facts on this boat trip. The boat travels through rooms that look like a rainforest, a desert, and a prairie. Then it heads to a modern greenhouse area.

A recording explains all the things your boat floats past. If you are lucky, you will see some giant vegetables growing here. The greenhouse has produced some of the biggest lemons and eggplants in the world.

In all, The Land grows more than 30 tons of fruit and veggies each year. A lot of it is served to guests in Epcot restaurants such as the Garden Grill and Coral Reef.

The Reader Review
 A Great Big Beautiful Day!

By: Sean, age 8
Schenectady, NY

I thought this ride was fun, and it taught me a lot about nature. I especially liked visiting the greenhouse. It was neat to see all sorts of plants from all around the world growing under one roof.

Soarin' Around the World

#10 RIDE PLEASER

FP+

Have you ever wondered what it's like to be a bird? To swoop and soar high above the clouds? This attraction lets you experience that first-hand. In it, you'll fly over natural wonders and famous buildings in India, China, Australia, the U.S.A., and more.

Fasten your safety belt

Before the fun starts, you will get a seat in one of the hang gliders. Put your stuff in the basket, fasten your seat belt, sit back, and get ready.

Up, up, and away!

As your glider lifts off the ground, a movie screen lights up in front of you. On it, you will see many different scenes. You'll swoop over oceans, countrysides, mountaintops. You will visit sites such as the Eiffel Tower and the Great Wall of China. You may even notice different smells along the way.

Many scenes were filmed using cameras on airplanes and helicopters. Your glider moves the same way those aircraft did — so it seems as if you are really flying.

How real does it feel? Some people lift their feet because they think their toes will hit the items below! The whole trip takes about five minutes. You must be at least 40 inches tall to ride. If you get motion sickness or are afraid of heights, skip this one.

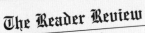
The Reader Review

By: Avery, age 8
Sloatsburg, NY
I love Soarin' because it feels like you're flying. You soar over beautiful views of real places and cute animals. I jumped when the whale popped out of the water! It was unexpected and it made me giggle.

Colortopia

Do you like to color? There is a special spot in Future World that is a celebration of color. There are three zones there: *The Power of Color* (a short movie that surrounds guests in a rainbow of colors); The Color Lab (where you can create colors); and Color Our World (where guests color with magic paintbrushes). This hands-on spot is in a building called Innoventions. It may not be open in all of 2019.

Imagination!

This pavilion is a workout for your imagination — the attractions really make you think. There is an interesting ride that tests your creativity and a hands-on activity center. Outside, the jumping waters of the Leap Frog Fountains are sure to cool you off and keep you guessing. There are a lot of other ways to have fun here, too. Just use your imagination!

Epcot

HOT TIP!

On a hot day, cool off by trying to catch the streams of water that jump from fountain to fountain at the entertaining Leap Frog Fountains.

Disney and Pixar Short Film Festival

The Magic Eye Theater is a bit unusual — its shows are in 4-D. The films are in 3-D and the theater has special "4-D" effects.

Before the action starts, guests watch a pre-show video. In it, Disney and Pixar artists explain how they create animation.

As you enter the theater, you'll pick up 3-D glasses. Put them on once you're safely settled in your seat.

The first of three short films is called *Get a Horse*. It's a wacky wagon-ride adventure starring Minnie, Mickey, and the rest of the gang. The other movies change from time to time, but they are sure to put a smile on your face. This is a nice place to escape the heat, rest your feet, and enjoy animated films.

Details may change in 2019. Check a park Times Guide to see which films will be shown during your visit to Epcot.

Journey Into Imagination with Figment

Think about how different the world would be without any imagination in it. There would be no stories to tell, no pictures to draw, and no inventions to make things easier. One thing is for sure — Walt Disney World would not exist! Imagination is so important to the folks at Disney that they made a special place in Future World to learn all about it. It is called the Imagination Institute — and it's having an open house. That means everyone is

invited to learn about all of its projects. And who better to take you on a tour of this special place than Figment himself? (Figment is a little purple dragon. He hosts this attraction. That's him in the picture. A lot of kids are Figment fans.)

As you exit the attraction, check out the Imageworks play zone. It has a couple of hands-on and feet-on activities. Games may change in 2019.

Epcot Character Spot

There are lots of places to meet Disney characters at Epcot. Do you want to know the best place? The Epcot Character Spot! It's near Fountain View and it is full of favorite characters. (The location may change in 2019.)

Of course, this is Epcot, so the characters greet you in specially themed areas. The themes may include transportation, space, land, and communication. If they sound familiar, it is because those are some of the themes that are featured in Epcot's Future World.

The characters take turns greeting guests throughout the day. Expect to find Disney pals like Mickey, Minnie, and Goofy. (Fastpass+ is available for them.) Of course, you never know who else might show up — so keep those cameras and the autograph section of this book handy. Afterward, head across the plaza to meet Baymax from *Big Hero 6*. *Inside Out*'s Joy and Sadness may be there, too.

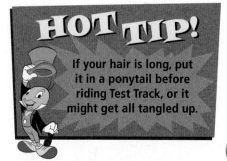

READER **#7 RIDE** PLEASER

FP+

Test Track

What is it like to create and test a car? Find out in this ride — and learn what it's like to make a new car that is as safe as can be.

Where are the brakes?

Test Track is one of Walt Disney World's fastest rides and Epcot's original thrill ride. After you design a car on a touch screen, you can test it on the track. Your car has no steering wheel or brake pedals for you to control, but its sound and video equipment let you know what's being tested. You zip around curves, zoom down a street, and reach a speed of 65 miles per hour. At one point, you nearly crash into a truck!

A crash course in car design

Kids think this ride is a fun way to learn all about cars. Parts of it are quite loud, so don't be startled if you hear a noisy crash. And don't worry — the ride is very safe. Disney workers tested all the cars first. After all, that's what test-driving is all about.

You must be at least 40 inches tall to try it. After the ride, check out the post-show area. It's pretty cool.

The Reader Review

By: Eric, age 12
Beverly Hills, CA

Test Track is the fastest, most surprising ride I have ever been on. I learned about car testing while having fun. I thought I would be scared, but I really enjoyed myself.

World Showcase

Anybody can be a world traveler — or a secret agent — at World Showcase. You can learn about many countries (including the U.S.A.), experience different cultures, and meet people from all over the world. You can also be a super spy and save the world in an interactive adventure — and even meet Anna and Elsa.

As you visit each of the countries, be sure to talk to the folks who work there. Most of the people in each pavilion really come from the country they represent. The pavilions were built around a lake called World Showcase Lagoon. If you make the trip all the way around the lake, you will walk more than one mile!

READER TIP

"There is a walking path and a big waterfall in the back of the Canada pavilion. It's super cool!"

Judy (age 10)
Greenwich, CT

HIDDEN MICKEY ALERT!
The iron grates that the trees in World Showcase grow out of could probably tell a mouse tale or two. They're covered with Hidden Mickeys!

Canada

If you look at a map of North America, Canada is at the top, just above the United States. It is a beautiful country. The Canada pavilion at Epcot is very pretty, too. There's a rocky mountain, a stream, gardens, and a totem pole.

The highlight is a movie called *O Canada!* The scenes completely surround you. Since you stand the whole time, it's easy to turn around and see everything. Many kids enjoy the movie but wish the theater had seats.

The Reader Review

By: Shelby, age 14
Calgary, Alberta, Canada

This pavilion shows what Canadians are proud of. I should know — I'm from Canada! I wish the film included even more, but it's a great introduction to my country.

United Kingdom

From London to the English countryside, this pavilion gives a varied view of the United Kingdom. Some details to look for include the smoke stains painted on the chimneys to make them appear old, and the grassy roofs that are really made of plastic broom bristles.

International Mouse

Mickey Mouse is famous all over the world. But not everyone knows the movie-star mouse by that name. In Italy he's called Topolino. In Greece he's known as Miky Maoye. Norwegians call him Mikke Mus. In Sweden he goes by Musse Pigg. And in China he's Mi Lao Shu. That's a lot of names for one mouse to remember!

France

The Eiffel Tower is probably the best-known landmark at the France pavilion. (The real one is in Paris, France.) The buildings here look just like those in a real French town. Many of the workers here come from France. They speak English with a French accent. Surprise them by saying *bonjour* (pronounced: *bohn-zhoor*). It means "good day" in French.

The main attraction — besides the treats at the bakery, an ice cream shop, and a chance to meet Belle — is a film called *Impressions de France.* The movie takes you from one end of France to the other. It's shown on a big screen, and you get to sit down and take in the sights.

Topiaries

PHOTO BY JILL SAFRO

There's something unusual about some of the trees and shrubs at Walt Disney World — they are shaped like Disney characters! These plants are called topiaries (pronounced: *TOE-pea-air-eez*). They are carefully grown by gardeners to create their special form. You may spot an Alice topiary by the Mad Tea Party in the Magic Kingdom, Mary Poppins at the Grand Floridian resort, and Sorcerer Mickey at the Disney Hollywood Studios' entrance. In the spring, Epcot has nearly 80 topiaries on display. How many can you find?

HOT TIP! Don't miss the special entertainment in each of the countries.

Morocco

The country of Morocco is famous for its mosaics — artwork and patterns that are made up of many tiles. That's why there is such beautiful tile work on the walls of this pavilion. Moroccan artists made sure the mosaics here were done right.

The buildings are copies of monuments in Moroccan cities, including Fez and Marrakesh. There are many shops selling items you could find in Morocco. You can buy baskets, brass, jewelry, sandals, a fez hat, and other Moroccan clothing.

A belly dancer may entertain guests at the Marrakesh restaurant. Princess Jasmine greets guests here, too.

Salaam alaikum (pronounced: *sah-LAHM wah-LAY-koom*) means "hello" in Morocco. (It's Arabic.)

READER TIP

"Try to eat meals early or late in the day to avoid long lines!"

John (age 14)
Washington Township, NJ

Japan

The giant temple out front is called a pagoda — and makes the Japanese pavilion easy to spot. It's modeled after a famous pagoda in the city of Nara, Japan.

Be sure to notice the evergreen trees. In Japan, they are symbols of eternal life. Some of the trees found in a traditional Japanese garden will not survive in Florida. Similar trees were used instead.

Japanese drummers often perform outside the pavilion. The huge department store has lots of souvenirs from Japan. Want to say "good morning" in Japanese? Just say *ohayo gozaimasu* (pronounced: *oh-hi-yoh goh-zy-ee-mahs*).

Just for Kids!

Epcot has something special for younger kids: Kidcot Fun Stops. There's one in each of the countries of World Showcase. At each of these spots, you can use crayons to color cutouts of Duffy the Disney Bear, make crafts, and learn how kids have fun in countries all over the world.

The American Adventure

The United States of America is the star of this pavilion. That's why it's called The American Adventure.

The American Adventure show takes place inside a building that looks a lot like Independence Hall (the real Independence Hall is in Philadelphia, Pennsylvania). The show celebrates the American spirit throughout U.S. history.

Benjamin Franklin and Mark Twain host the show. (Ben Franklin is one of the founders of the U.S.A. And Mark Twain is one of its greatest authors.) They look so real, you may forget that they are mechanical. Ben Franklin even walks up stairs!

The American Adventure show honors many heroes from history: the pilgrims, Alexander Graham Bell, Jackie Robinson, Susan B. Anthony, Walt Disney, and others. It's a great way to learn about American history. It's best for older kids.

The Reader Review

By: Joshua, age 12
Cheektowaga, NY

The American Adventure is educational yet very entertaining. It is impossible to leave without a smile on your face and a true feeling of pride for being an American.

HIDDEN MICKEY ALERT!
Look closely at the fireworks behind the Statue of Liberty (in the American Adventure attraction). One burst leaves a Mickey-shaped puff of smoke.

Italy

Venice is an Italian city known for waterways called canals. There are no big canals at Epcot's Italy, but the pavilion does look a lot like the real thing. The tower is a smaller version of the Campanile, a famous building in Venice.

Notice the gondolas (pronounced: *GAHN-doe-lahz*) tied to the dock in the lagoon. They are a type of boat used for traveling in the canals of Venice.

Say *buon giorno* (pronounced: *bwon JOR-no*). It means "good day" in Italian.

Germany

HIDDEN MICKEY ALERT!
You'll find a Mickey in the grass in Germany's miniature village.

There isn't a village in Germany quite like the one at Epcot. It's a combination of cities and small towns from all around the country. Try to stop by the pavilion on the hour so you can see the special cuckoo clock near the toy shop and hear it chime.

In German, "good day" is *guten tag* (say: *GOO-ten tahg*).

The Reader Review

A Great Big Beautiful Day!

By: Micheline, age 9
Coral Springs, FL

Germany is one of my favorite pavilions. I love the cuckoo clocks, teddy bears, and sausages. A great time to visit Germany is in October for Oktoberfest. There are special games, food, singing, and dancing.

China

Disney's version of the Temple of Heaven is at the center of this pavilion. It's a landmark in the Chinese city of Beijing. Inside, there is a Circle-Vision 360 movie called *Reflections of China.* (There are no seats in the theater.)

Before going in to watch the movie, take a look at the waiting area. It's decorated in shades of red and gold. These colors mean good luck in China.

The film takes guests on a tour of the country. It's worth seeing, but it is more popular with adults than kids. Most kids would rather spend their time checking out the fish in the koi pond or watching the acrobats perform in the courtyard.

To say "hello" in Chinese, say *ni hao* (pronounced: *nee HOW*).

The Reader Review

A Great Big Beautiful Day!

By: Beckie, age 9
Gettysburg, PA

I really like Epcot's China. It has a massive gift shop, a pond with fish, and lots of food, plus a movie! I could spend a year — and a lot of money — here.

HOT TIP!

Get a Fastpass for the *Frozen* boat ride — or get there as the attraction opens.

FP+

Norway

You will discover the history and culture of Norway at this pavilion. The magical kingdom of Arendelle can be discovered here, too!

The main building is a castle. It was based on an ancient fortress in Norway's capital city of Oslo. Inside, there is an attraction called Frozen Ever After. On this boat ride, guests travel through the beautiful (and icy) Arendelle. It includes a Summer Celebration and a visit to Elsa's Ice Palace. Expect to see friends from *Frozen* — including Anna, Elsa, Kristoff, Olaf, and Sven.

Frozen is a popular movie — and this is a very popular attraction. Get a Fastpass if you can. The ride is fun for guests of all ages.

Saying "hello" is easy in Norway. It's *hallo!*

Epcot

Meet Anna and Elsa!

What do Anna and Elsa do when they are not building snowmen or preparing for Coronation Day? They greet guests at the Royal Sommerhus in Epcot's Norway pavilion! Come to this building with a camera and autograph book ready. (You can use the pages at the back of this book for autographs.)

People from around the world come to meet these royal sisters. Fastpass is offered for the experience, and assignments run out far in advance. The standby line can be quite long — but for many *Frozen* fans it is worth the wait.

FP+

Phineas and Ferb: Agent P's World Showcase Adventure

How would you like to become a secret agent and help Perry the Platypus fight evil scientist Dr. Heinz Doofenshmirtz? Here's your chance! The interactive game is based on the Disney Channel show *Phineas and Ferb*. Of course, you don't have to know the show to have fun playing along here. Before you start, head to the World Showcase part of Epcot. Then go to *www.agentpwsa.com* on a smartphone or tablet. (Be sure to get a parent's permission first.) Once you've signed up, it's time to pick your mission.

There are 6 different pavilions in which to play: Mexico, China, Germany, Japan, France, and the United Kingdom. Each pavilion offers a different mission — it's fun to complete them all.

There is no charge to play, but wireless data rates may apply. Grown-ups enjoy this game, too — so invite your parents to join in. Agent P's World Showcase Adventure may be replaced with a new game in 2019.

Epcot

HIDDEN MICKEY ALERT!
The volcano at the beginning of the boat ride is about to erupt! Watch the swirling smoke carefully and you might spot that famous mouse.

Mexico

The pyramid building at the Mexico pavilion is home to an attraction called Gran Fiesta Tour Starring the Three Caballeros. It is a boat trip that takes you through the country of Mexico.

The Three Caballeros are José, Panchito, and Donald (Duck, that is). They starred in a movie together way back in 1944. Now they're back together and planning to do a big show in Mexico City. But there is a problem. Donald keeps getting lost! Don't worry, there is a happy ending. This is Disney World, after all.

After the ride, you may get to meet Donald Duck. He greets guests just outside the pyramid. (He moves inside when the weather is rainy.) You may also catch a performance by a musical group called Mariachi Cobre. The 12-piece band plays traditional Mexican songs.

"Hello" here is *hola* (say: *OH-lah*).

Entertainment

Epcot is known for its awesome entertainment. There are lots of shows and special performances every day of the year. For more information, check a park Times Guide.

ILLUMINATIONS: REFLECTIONS OF EARTH

An amazing fireworks show takes place each night on and around World Showcase Lagoon. It tells the story of Earth's history. You can get a good view of it from anywhere around the lagoon.

The Reader Review

A Great Big Beautiful Day!

By: Jordan, age 14
Maynard, MA

IllumiNations is absolutely beautiful. It's a great way of telling the story of Earth's history. You can get a good view from anywhere around the lagoon, but I like to watch from the United Kingdom.

JAMMITORS

One of the loudest and wildest shows is inside Future World, where musicians bang out rhythms on trash cans and, sometimes, on one another. It's a blast!

WORLD SHOWCASE PERFORMERS

There is live entertainment at each of the pavilions in World Showcase. Highlights include a rock band called the British Revolution in the United Kingdom, acrobats in France, drummers in Japan, and much more. A group called The Voices of Liberty sings patriotic songs in the American Adventure pavilion. Feel free to clap and sing along.

Where to find
Characters
at EPCOT

A great place to meet Disney characters is at the **Epcot Character Spot** in Future World. Friends such as Mickey, Minnie, and Goofy take turns visiting with guests there throughout the day. Baymax, Joy, and Sadness are nearby. And they are always happy to sign autographs and pose for photos. (Baymax doesn't sign, but he loves to pose!)

You may also run into characters from Disney while wandering around the **World Showcase** section of the park. They tend to show up during the morning and afternoon. Don't forget to ask the characters to sign the autograph section of this book.

Epcot Tips

Start your day at Test Track or Frozen Ever After, followed by Soarin' Around the World and your preferred version of Mission: SPACE. Then say hi to Nemo at The Seas with Nemo and Friends. Next, head to the Imagination pavilion.

Remember: Most of World Showcase usually opens at 11 A.M.

Need a refreshing splash? Visit Cool Wash by Test Track, the squirting sidewalk that leads to World Showcase, or the fountain by Mission: SPACE.

Go to Spaceship Earth later in the day. That is when the line for the attraction is usually the shortest.

Each World Showcase country has its own special Duffy stamp. Ask for one at the Kidcot Fun Stop in each country. You can collect the stamps on the last page of this book.

Spaceship Earth, Mission: SPACE, and Journey Into Imagination with Figment all have post-show activity zones. You can play in them even if you skip the attractions themselves.

Bring Disney pins with you so you will have something to trade with Cast Members (workers) throughout Walt Disney World. Get a parent's permission before you trade anything.

Try not to squeeze the movies at Canada, France, and China all into one day.

Take time to talk to the people who work in World Showcase. Most of them come from the country of the pavilion they represent, and they have many interesting stories to tell.

You can sample soda for free at Club Cool. It's in Future World (near The Fountain of Nations).

Attraction Ratings

COOL
(Check It Out)

- China (This pavilion has a movie about China.)
- Italy
- France (This pavilion has a movie about France.)
- United Kingdom
- Morocco
- Germany
- Japan
- Norway

REALLY COOL
(Don't Miss)

- The American Adventure
- Disney and Pixar Short Film Festival
- Journey Into Imagination with Figment
- Gran Fiesta Tour
- Canada (This pavilion has a movie about Canada.)
- Living with the Land
- Mexico
- Colortopia

THE COOLEST
(See at least twice)

- Frozen Ever After
- Soarin' Around the World
- Test Track
- Turtle Talk with Crush
- Mission: SPACE
- Spaceship Earth
- The Seas with Nemo and Friends
- IllumiNations

Your favorite Epcot attractions

_____

_____

_____

_____

_____

_____

Disney's Hollywood Studios

Disney's Hollywood Studios lets you experience imaginary worlds from movies and TV shows. There are attractions that let you ride a Slinky Dog roller coaster, sing along with Anna and Elsa, learn how to use the Force to defeat the Dark Side, see how wild stunts are performed, and a whole lot more.

The Studios park looks a little like Hollywood did back in the 1940s. Hollywood is the California city where movie-making got its big start. Disney's Hollywood Studios park got its big start in 1989. It has shows and attractions based on *Frozen, Toy Story, Star Wars, The Twilight Zone*, The Muppets, and other favorites.

You will also get to meet lots of characters, including Mickey, Minnie, Buzz, Woody, and the stars of Disney's newest films and shows — be sure to bring a pen for autographs. There are new attractions planned for this park — and some older ones will be going away. One thing is for sure: There are plenty of surprises in store!

Use this map to explore Disney's Hollywood Studios theme park.

A Beauty and the Beast — Live on Stage

B Fantasmic!

C The Twilight Zone Tower of Terror

D Rock 'n' Roller Coaster

E Star Wars Launch Bay

F Disney Junior — Live on Stage!

G Walt Disney Presents

H Voyage of The Little Mermaid

I Toy Story Midway Mania!

J Muppet∗Vision 3-D

K Star Tours — The Adventures Continue

L Indiana Jones Epic Stunt Spectacular

M Mickey & Minnie's Runaway Railway

N For the First Time in Forever: A Frozen Sing-Along Celebration

O Slinky Dog Dash

P Alien Swirling Saucers

Sunset Blvd.

Animation Courtyard

Toy Story Land

Hollywood Blvd.

Grand Avenue

Echo Lake

Bus Transportation

Walt Disney World Resort Guest Boat Transportation

The Twilight Zone™ Tower of Terror

At a height of 199 feet, Tower of Terror is one of the tallest attractions at Walt Disney World. For some people, it is also the scariest.

Legend says that one Halloween night, lightning hit The Hollywood Tower Hotel. A whole section of the hotel disappeared! So did an elevator carrying five people. No one ever saw them again.

Haunted hotel

Now the hotel is haunted. If you dare to enter it, you are in for a few surprises. First, you walk through the dusty hotel lobby. Then you enter a tiny room, where Rod Serling appears on TV. (He was the host of a spooky show called *The Twilight Zone*.) Once Rod tells you the story of The Hollywood Tower Hotel, get ready — you are on your way to the Twilight Zone.

#6 RIDE PLEASER

Going down!

After waiting in the boiler room, you are given a seat in a big elevator. The elevator takes you on a short tour of the hotel, where you see some special effects. But the highlight comes when the elevator cables snap. *Whoosh!* You plunge eight stories! Next, the elevator shoots up to the hotel's 13th floor. It teeters for a moment and then . . . it drops again and again at blazing speed! You must be at least 40 inches tall to ride.

Disney's Hollywood Studios

WILD Attraction Reaction

LOUD Attraction Reaction

DARK Attraction Reaction

SCARY Attraction Reaction

Rock 'n' Roller Coaster Starring Aerosmith

 FP+

READER #3 RIDE PLEASER

This ride rocks! It travels at top speed and flips you upside down three times. It also has a rock 'n' roll soundtrack that will have you dancing in your seat.

You're invited

Rock 'n' Roller Coaster goes really fast — it takes you from zero to 60 miles per hour in the first three seconds of the ride! You need the speed because you're on your way to a party at an Aerosmith concert — and you're running late.

It's showtime!

The ride takes place in a stretch limousine on a roller coaster track. The limo's radio is tuned to the concert. You can hear the band warming up, but your car is not moving yet. Then, just as the concert starts, the light turns green and you're on your way. You zoom along the California highway and make it just in time for the end of the show. Hang on!

You must be at least 48 inches tall to ride Rock 'n' Roller Coaster.

The Reader Review A Great Big Beautiful Day!

By: Jayden, age 8
Orlando, FL

Three, two, one — let's rock! This is a super fast roller coaster. It even goes upside down! Don't go if you are afraid of the dark or don't like going fast.

Beauty and the Beast — Live on Stage

It's hard to keep quiet during this stage show — it makes you want to clap and sing along. The music comes straight from Disney's animated film *Beauty and the Beast.*

As the show begins, Belle is frustrated by life in her small town. She is dreaming of exciting, faraway places. Later on, she becomes a prisoner in the Beast's castle. All of the castle's residents are under a magic spell. Lumiere, Cogsworth, Mrs. Potts, and the rest of the gang are there to help Belle (and perform "Be Our Guest"). In the end, the spell is broken. The Beast becomes human again.

Read a park Times Guide for schedules and updates. You can get a free Times Guide in many shops in the park. Just ask.

The Reader Review

By: Pharra, age 11
Alpharetta, GA

I liked the lively colors and the music in this show. I didn't like how it skipped so fast from one song to the next, because that made it more challenging to follow along, but I still got the story. It's a show the entire family can enjoy!

HOT TIP!

The sidewalk by The Chinese Theater is covered with handprints and footprints. They belong to famous performers. Put your palms and feet in the prints and compare yours with the stars'. (Wash your hands when you are done.)

HIDDEN MICKEY ALERT!

Mickey Mouse is one of the Hollywood stars whose footprints and handprints are on the sidewalk in front of The Chinese Theater!

Mickey & Minnie's Runaway Railway

How many cartoons have you seen in your lifetime? Hundreds? Thousands? Well, how many have you actually been in? Probably not too many! This new attraction puts you in the middle of wild and wacky Mickey Mouse cartoons.

HOT TIP!

Mickey & Minnie's Runaway Railway is expected to open in 2019. Will the ride be open during your trip to Walt Disney World? Visit *mydisneyexperience.com* (with a parent) to find out!

You're a star

At Mickey & Minnie's Runaway Railway, you'll go *through* the screen and feel like you're part of the show. Of course, you won't be alone in the crazy cartoon world — lots of Disney friends will join you on the journey.

All aboard!

The adventure begins with Mickey and Minnie preparing for a picnic. Then — *TOOT, TOOT!* A train chugs up and Goofy is the engineer. That's when you join the fun. Anything can happen in the cartoon world, so expect lots of surprises. This attraction will not be open in all of 2019.

For the First Time in Forever: A Frozen Sing-Along Celebration

Have you ever heard of a song called "Let It Go"? Yes, we thought so! That is just one of the many musical numbers in the movie *Frozen*. And this is the spot to go to if you want to sing along with the characters in the film.

Singing in Arendelle

The interactive experience happens in the park's Hyperion Theater. The show begins with Arendelle getting two new historians. They retell the *Frozen* story and ask the audience to sing along when film clips play on a giant screen. Don't know all the words? Just follow the bouncing snowflake.

Anna and Elsa take the stage!

Singing with the movie is fun, but many kids think the best part is when Anna and Elsa appear live on stage. Check a Times Guide for the show schedule. And get there early.

Who am I?

- I live in Arendelle.
- I don't have a skull. Or bones.
- Warm hugs make me happy.

Answer: Olaf

Disney Junior — Live on Stage!

Are you a Disney Junior fan? If so, head straight to this attraction. Friends from Disney Junior programs will dazzle you in a colorful show. Expect to find characters from *Mickey Mouse Clubhouse*, *Doc McStuffins*, *Sofia the First*, *Jake and the Never Land Pirates*, and more.

Have a seat on the floor!

When you walk into the theater, you will notice something unusual about it — there are no seats. But do not worry. The carpet is comfy, so sit down and make yourself at home. (There are a few benches in the back of the theater. Grown-ups like to sit on them.)

A big hit with little guests

Big kids may get a kick out of Disney Junior — Live on Stage, but younger kids seem to have the most fun here. If you have little brothers or sisters, be sure to bring them to this show.

Some parts of this show may change in 2019.

Mickey and Minnie Starring in Red Carpet Dreams

It's no secret that Mickey Mouse and Minnie Mouse are big Hollywood stars. And they have invited you to meet them backstage at Disney's Hollywood Studios — at a special building on Commissary Lane. Inside, Minnie looks like she is ready for a fancy party or awards show. Mickey is decked out in his magical outfit from *Fantasia*. (In that film, he plays the Sorcerer's Apprentice.)

Both mice are happy to greet their fans, pose for photos, and sign autographs — because that's what friendly Hollywood stars do! Check a Times Guide for their schedule on the day you visit the park.

HIDDEN MICKEY ALERT!

Lasers at the start of the show form a Mickey head.

Disney's Hollywood Studios

Voyage of The Little Mermaid

You don't have to be a fish to have fun underwater — and this show proves it. In it, you go below the ocean's surface with Ariel and her friends from *The Little Mermaid*. They sing and act out the story on a stage. Ariel and Eric star along with puppets, including Flounder, Sebastian, and other sea creatures.

Under the sea

There are some special effects that draw you into the show. A screen of water makes it seem like the theater really is under the sea. Lasers flash, lightning strikes, and mist sprays the audience. Scenes from the movie are shown on a big screen behind the stage.

A winning combination

The combination of people, puppets, and special effects makes for a nice show. To get the best view of all the action, try sitting toward the back of the theater. From there, the puppets look like they are really swimming.

Big changes are coming to this theme park. Some attractions — including this one — may close in 2019 to make way for new ones.

Walt Disney Presents

You probably know a lot about Mickey Mouse — he has a pup named Pluto, he loves red shorts, and Minnie Mouse is his favorite gal. But how much do you know about the man who created him? You can learn a lot about Walt Disney at this attraction. He's the man who started The Walt Disney Company.

Take your time

Lots of Walt's belongings are on display here. Look for special items like Disney family photos, his piano, and the Academy Award he won for *Snow White and the Seven Dwarfs*. Spend some time exploring the exhibits before you see the film about Walt.

Fun fact

Did you know that Mickey Mouse wasn't Walt's first famous cartoon character? A rabbit named Oswald was. But Walt's plans for Oswald didn't quite work out. Luckily, he never gave up, or he never would have created Mickey!

To learn more about Walt Disney, turn to page 8 of this book.

The Reader Review

A Great Big Beautiful Day!

By: Jennifer, age 12
Salina, KS

This is a wonderful exhibit. It really helps you get to know Walt Disney and the magic that he brought to the world.

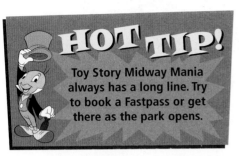

HOT TIP!

Toy Story Midway Mania always has a long line. Try to book a Fastpass or get there as the park opens.

Toy Story Midway Mania!

If you think Buzz Lightyear's Space Ranger Spin is a blast, you will love Toy Story Midway Mania! It's like jumping into a life-size video game. It also makes you feel like you're the size of a toy as you travel through colorful rooms and stop in front of screens filled with targets.

This high-tech ride has a twist: All guests wear 3-D glasses. That makes all of the special effects really pop. As you rack up points and trigger surprises, you'll be cheered on by Woody, Buzz, Jessie, Rex, Hamm, and lots of other Toy Story stars.

Toy Story Midway Mania is good for gamers of all ages and skill levels. So if you are a beginner, you'll get better each time you play. In fact, we're pretty sure you will be giving pointers to your parents.

#8 RIDE
READER PLEASER

Disney's Hollywood Studios

The Reader Review

A Great Big Beautiful Day!

By: Tyler, age 13
Corona City, CA

I love this ride! All the hidden ways to score points and competing against others make it more fun. It's good for all ages. LOVE this ride.

PHOTO BY JILL SAFRO

Slinky Dog Dash

If you've seen the movie *Toy Story*, you know that Andy is a very creative kid. But did you know he could build a roller coaster? Yep, Andy used his trusty roller coaster kit to build Slinky Dog Dash — a new attraction in the park's Toy Story Land.

Andy's creation lets guests ride in a car that looks exactly

like Slinky Dog. The cars dash along a brightly colored track that twists around Andy's backyard. This adventure is much tamer than Rock 'N' Roller Coaster, but it's still a ride on the wild side. Guests of all ages enjoy it. You must be at least 32 inches tall to ride Slinky Dog Dash.

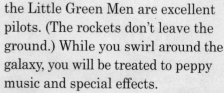

Alien Swirling Saucers

Andy won a space-toy playset at the Pizza Planet Arcade — and he wants to share it with YOU. Just climb inside a rocket-shaped toy and get ready to swirl. The rocket will be pulled by a flying saucer and an alien from Toy Story. Don't worry —

the Little Green Men are excellent pilots. (The rockets don't leave the ground.) While you swirl around the galaxy, you will be treated to peppy music and special effects.

Guests must be at least 30 inches tall to experience this swirling ride.

HOT TIP!

The Indiana Jones Epic Stunt Spectacular is a noisy show! If explosions and other loud noises hurt your ears, sit in the back of the theater. It's not as loud there.

READER TIP

"Outside of Indiana Jones, there is a sign that says: DO NOT PULL THE ROPE. Ignore the sign and pull that rope! You'll be glad you did."

Cameron (age 10)
Naples, FL

Indiana Jones Epic Stunt Spectacular

Fire, explosions, daring escapes, and other special effects are the stars of this attraction. Stunt men and stunt women act out scenes from the movie *Raiders of the Lost Ark* and show how special effects are done. The audience watches from a large theater, and adults are chosen to perform with the pros. (It is too dangerous for kids.)

Fun for everyone

All the surprises keep everyone on the edge of their seats. One of the best parts of the show is the re-creation of a scene in the movie where a giant boulder rolls down and seems to crush Indiana Jones.

Even though you know it's a stunt, it seems quite real.

Don't try this at home

Expert stunt people act out the scenes and then explain how each of the stunts was performed. They make it look easy, but it is not. Don't try this at home!

The Reader Review

A Great Big Beautiful Day!

By: Philip, age 11
Palm Harbor, FL

This is great for anyone who likes stunts, action, adventure, and Indiana Jones movies. It's my favorite show at Walt Disney World.

Muppet✳Vision 3-D

Don't miss this attraction — it is one of the park's funniest. It begins with a wacky pre-show starring Fozzie Bear, Gonzo, Scooter, and Sam Eagle. Then you go into a special theater that looks just like the one from Jim Henson's *The Muppet Show*. Here, you will see 3-D movie effects mixed with some other special tricks.

Amazing effects

Some of the effects are so good that it's hard to tell what's part of the movie and what's real. During Miss Piggy's big song, bubbles look like they are just inches away from you. Don't be surprised if they really are.

Look around the theater

Be sure to look all around you when you're watching the show. Some of the best action happens off the screen. Try to keep an eye out for the Swedish Chef. He is cooking up a plan in the back of the theater.

The Reader Review

By: Carrie, age 13
Hinsdale, IL

This is an all-around great show. I recommend it to everyone! The characters in the movie come right out at you, and you feel like you could reach out and touch them. It's very cool!

DISNEY FASTPASS+ ENTRANCE

STAR TOURS

STAND-BY ENTRANCE
WAIT TIME
MINUTES

HOT TIP!

There are about 50 different versions of Star Tours, so each adventure is a surprise!

READER TIP

"Star Tours really pulls you around and shakes you up. Be prepared for a wild ride!"

Kinsey (age 7)
Athens, GA

Star Tours — The Adventures Continue

If you've ever been to Star Tours before, you should come back soon — it's a little different almost every time. The journey through the galaxy makes guests feel like they are part of a Star Wars movie. Before the trip, be sure to put on the special glasses — this adventure is in 3-D. Keep your eye out for Princess Leia, Darth Vader, Yoda, Finn, and BB-8.

It feels real

The ride takes place on a flight simulator, the same type used to train astronauts and pilots. The combination of the simulator and movie makes it feel like you are really rocketing through space.

Hang on tight

The Star Tours adventure has sharp turns and lots of bumpy thrills. Don't eat anything just before you enter the attraction.

You must be at least 40 inches tall to experience Star Tours.

FP+

The Reader Review

A Great Big Beautiful Day!

By: Lily, age 11
Bullard, TX

This is fun for kids who love Star Wars, as well as those who have never seen it. The 3-D attraction is fun for children of all ages — and it's wonderful to ride with Star Wars–loving parents.

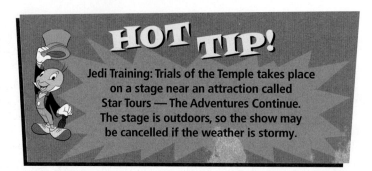

HOT TIP!

Jedi Training: Trials of the Temple takes place on a stage near an attraction called Star Tours — The Adventures Continue. The stage is outdoors, so the show may be cancelled if the weather is stormy.

Jedi Training: Trials of the Temple

Calling all Padawans — you can become a Junior Jedi and defend the galaxy at Jedi Training: Trials of the Temple. It is open to kids between the ages of 4 and 12. All trainees wear brown Jedi robes and recite the Jedi Oath. They also learn how to use the Force to wield a lightsaber. A Jedi Master shares tricks and teaches Junior Jedi Knights how to defend against the Dark Side.

If you just want to watch the lesson, check a park Times Guide and head to the stage a few minutes before showtime. If you want to be in the show, sign up at the Indiana Jones Adventure Outpost. (It is between the Indiana Jones Epic Stunt Spectacular and the 50's Prime Time Cafe.) You should arrive very early in the day to reserve a spot in Jedi Training: Trials of the Temple. May the Force be with you!

After the performance, all robes and lightsabers are returned to the Jedi Master. Each show lasts about 20 minutes.

Stormtrooper March

If you hear the sound of marching footsteps, you may want to get out of the way — Captain Phasma leads a march of Stormtroopers down the park's Hollywood Boulevard. Guests are welcome to join the march and follow behind the First Order. Just don't give in to the Dark Side! The Stormtrooper March takes place daily. Check a park Times Guide for the schedule during your visit to Disney's Hollywood Studios.

HOT TIP!

Star Wars: A Galaxy Far, Far Away is a stage show that takes place on Hollywood Boulevard. It is presented several times each day. Check a park Times Guide for the schedule.

Star Wars Launch Bay

The Launch Bay is a walk-through attraction that celebrates the stories and characters of the Star Wars universe. At the entrance, guests may head to the Launch Bay Theater. There guests view a film about Star Wars movies. It's a look at old favorites and a peek into the future.

Look at that lightsaber

Parts of the Launch Bay are like a museum filled with props, costumes, and other Star Wars items. Guests enjoy a close-up look at Stormtrooper helmets, lightsabers, and more. There's a spider bike from *Return of the Jedi* and a copy of Rey's speeder from *The Force Awakens*.

PHOTO BY JILL SAFRO

Meet Chewie

Launch Bay also has a space to meet characters from Star Wars movies. Would you like to meet Chewbacca, BB-8, or Kylo Ren? Here's your chance! (Characters may take turns throughout the day.)

Details may change in 2019.

Star Wars: Galaxy's Edge

There's a brand-new land coming to Disney's Hollywood Studios! It is called Star Wars: Galaxy's Edge. As the story goes, a distant planet called Batuu was once a very busy place for space traders. These days it's mostly visited by explorers, smugglers, and folks trying to avoid the First Order. Soon it will welcome Disney park guests, too.

When it opens, Galaxy's Edge will have two major Star Wars–themed adventures. One attraction lets guests pilot the Millennium Falcon spaceship and complete a very important mission. The other attraction makes guests feel as if they are in the middle of a battle between the First Order and the Resistance. Pretty intense!

Of course, the area will also have entertainment, shops, character meet-and-greets, and awesome eats. If you've seen the movie *Star Wars IV: A New Hope*, you know that Luke Skywalker enjoys drinking blue milk. We think Luke will be happy to hear that he can get blue milk in Star Wars: Galaxy's Edge! For more information, visit *www.disneyworld.com*.

HOT TIP!

The opening date for Star Wars: Galaxy's Edge is not so far, far away. The new land may be open in late 2019 or early 2020. For updates, use the My Disney Experience mobile app or website, or visit *www.disneyworld.com*. (Be sure to get a parent's permission.)

Who am I?

- I used to be called Dippy Dog.
- My hat is green.
- Max is my son.

Answer: Goofy

Entertainment

Lights! Camera! Action! There's a lot of cool entertainment at Disney's Hollywood Studios. Most of it has a TV or movie theme. Some of the best shows are described below.

CITIZENS OF HOLLYWOOD

If you take a walk on this park's Hollywood or Sunset boulevard, you might run into performers called Citizens of Hollywood. They play the parts of movie stars, policemen, cab drivers, reporters, and other funny characters from the 1930s and 1940s. They love to talk to theme park guests, so don't be shy. You will feel like you are a part of the show.

FANTASMIC!

What does Mickey Mouse dream about? You can find out at Fantasmic! It's an amazing show that combines water, laser lights, Disney characters, movies, music, and a little magic.

Mickey's dreams are fun to watch — but some of them are a little scary. (Disney villains keep turning his dreams into nightmares.) In the end, good wins over evil, and Mickey's dreams are happy once more.

Fantasmic is presented in a theater beside a lake near the Tower of Terror. It's very popular, so be sure to line up at least an hour before the show starts. And, if it isn't summer, bring a jacket or a sweater — it can get chilly. If you sit near the front, you might get a little bit wet. The lake gets lit on fire, too. Check a park Times Guide to see what nights Fantasmic is performed.

STAR WARS: A GALACTIC SPECTACULAR

The park ends some nights with a fireworks display on Hollywood Boulevard. The Star Wars–themed show has bursts of color, lively music, and some very special effects. The galactic spectacular is presented during busy times of year. It may not take place during your visit to the park.

Where to find
Characters
at DISNEY'S HOLLYWOOD STUDIOS

There are lots of places to meet Disney and Pixar characters at Disney's Hollywood Studios. Mickey and Minnie Mouse greet folks in separate rooms at **Mickey and Minnie Starring in Red Carpet Dreams.** You will find everyone's favorite snowman, Olaf, in the nearby **Celebrity Spotlight** building.

Pluto and Disney Junior characters such as Doc McStuffins, Jake (from *Jake and the Never Land Pirates*), and Sofia the First appear in **Animation Courtyard.** Friends and foes from Star Wars like to hang out inside **Star Wars Launch Bay.** Stormtroopers have been known to march (and pose for photos) in the area near **Mickey and Minnie's Runaway Railway** (a new attraction that is expected to open in 2019).

Jessie, Woody, and Buzz greet park guests in **Toy Story Land.** Ask them to sign the autograph section at the end of this book. You might spot a Green Army Man there, too.

Details may change in 2019.

Disney's Hollywood Studios

Arrive at Disney's Hollywood Studios before the opening time. The gates often open a few minutes ahead of the scheduled time.

Bring this book to the park. When you meet Disney characters, you'll have something for them to sign!

There are "chicken exits" at both Tower of Terror and Rock 'n' Roller Coaster, just in case you change your mind at the last minute.

Don't eat before you ride Rock 'n' Roller Coaster, Slinky Dog Dash, Star Tours, Alien Swirling Saucers, or Twilight Zone Tower of Terror.

Some stage shows don't open until late morning. Be sure to check a Times Guide for exact show times.

Some folks think the number 13 is scary. But if the wait time at Tower of Terror is listed as 13 minutes, there is probably a much shorter wait — and that's not scary at all!

A new land is coming to this park! For details about Star Wars — Galaxy's Edge, visit *mydisneyexperience.com*.

The front rows at Fantasmic get a little wet. The best seats are in the back at either end of the theater.

Expect the attractions in Toy Story Land and Galaxy's Edge (once the new land has opened) to be quite popular. Get Fastpasses whenever you can!

Attraction Ratings

COOL
(Check It Out)

- Disney Junior — Live on Stage!
- Walt Disney Presents
- Jedi Training: Trials of the Temple
- Star Wars Launch Bay
- Star Wars: A Galaxy Far, Far Away (show)
- Stormtrooper March

REALLY COOL
(Don't Miss)

- Alien Swirling Saucers
- Beauty and the Beast — Live on Stage
- For the First Time in Forever: A Frozen Sing-Along Celebration
- Indiana Jones Epic Stunt Spectacular
- Fantasmic!
- Muppet*Vision 3-D
- Voyage of The Little Mermaid

THE COOLEST
(See at least twice)

- Toy Story Midway Mania!
- Slinky Dog Dash
- The Twilight Zone Tower of Terror
- Mickey and Minnie's Runaway Railway (opening in late 2019)
- Rock 'n' Roller Coaster Starring Aerosmith
- Star Tours — The Adventures Continue
- Star Wars: A Galactic Spectacular (fireworks)

Your favorite Disney's Hollywood Studios attractions

Disney's Animal Kingdom

PHOTO BY MIKE CARROLL

Animal Kingdom celebrates animals of every kind, from lions, tigers, and zebras to giant turtles whose ancestors lived during the time of the dinosaurs. And they're all real! You may get closer to them than you've ever been before. There are dinosaurs, too. The dinos aren't real, but they sure seem to be.

Animal Kingdom is a theme park with many attractions. Just like the Magic Kingdom, there are different "lands" to visit in Animal Kingdom. The major lands are called Discovery Island, Asia, Africa, DinoLand U.S.A., and Pandora — The World of Avatar.

You enter the park through The Oasis. It's a big garden with plants and animals. Take some time to look around. Then cross a bridge to Discovery Island, admire the giant Tree of Life, and decide which land to explore first.

What's the best way to see Animal Kingdom? Use this map to help you decide!

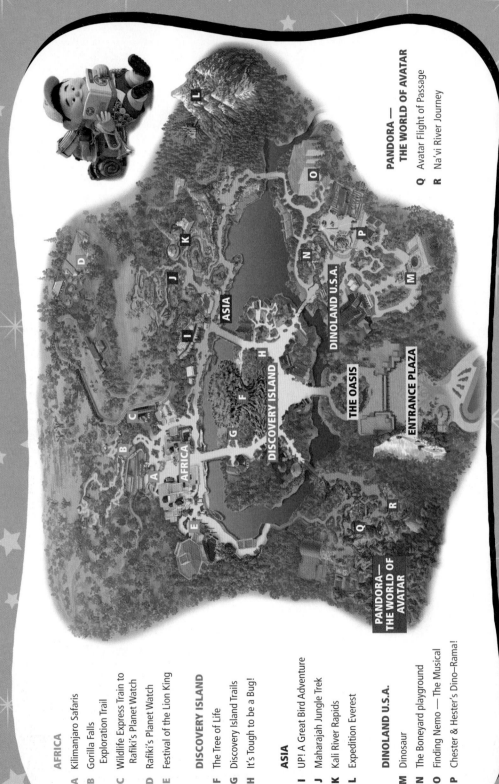

AFRICA

- **A** Kilimanjaro Safaris
- **B** Gorilla Falls Exploration Trail
- **C** Wildlife Express Train to Rafiki's Planet Watch
- **D** Rafiki's Planet Watch
- **E** Festival of the Lion King

DISCOVERY ISLAND

- **F** The Tree of Life
- **G** Discovery Island Trails
- **H** It's Tough to be a Bug!

ASIA

- **I** UP! A Great Bird Adventure
- **J** Maharajah Jungle Trek
- **K** Kali River Rapids
- **L** Expedition Everest

DINOLAND U.S.A.

- **M** Dinosaur
- **N** The Boneyard playground
- **O** Finding Nemo — The Musical
- **P** Chester & Hester's Dino-Rama!

PANDORA — THE WORLD OF AVATAR

- **Q** Avatar Flight of Passage
- **R** Na'vi River Journey

Discovery Island

Discovery Island is the gateway to all the other lands in the park. The Tree of Life stands near the center of Discovery Island. If you wander near its roots, you will see many different kinds of creatures.

HIDDEN MICKEY ALERT!

There's a mouse in the moss! Look for clusters of moss near the tiger on The Tree of Life. They form a Hidden Mickey.

PHOTO BY MIKE CARROLL

Disney's Animal Kingdom

The Tree of Life

This human-made tree is 145 feet tall. From far away it looks like any other tree. But when you get up close, you'll see that this is not an ordinary tree. It's covered with animals!

Artists have carved 325 animal images into its trunk. In fact, it's called The Tree of Life because it's covered with so many different kinds of animal life. The lion is easy to see. Other animals, such as the ant and dolphin, are a lot harder to spot. How many can you find?

The Reader Review

A Great Big Beautiful Day!

By: John, age 14
Washington Township, NJ

Once inside Animal Kingdom, you can't miss The Tree of Life. Trying to spot all the animals on the tree is nearly impossible! A great place to search for animals is while in line for It's Tough to be a Bug!

"At It's Tough to be a Bug, be sure to sit back straight in your chair so you don't miss a thing."

Chelsea (age 12)
Howell, NJ

HOT TIP!

If you hate creepy crawlers, skip It's Tough to be a Bug!

Disney's Animal Kingdom

PHOTO BY JILL SAFRO

It's Tough to be a Bug!

The Tree of Life has a hollow trunk. It's cool, dark, and roomy inside. That makes it a great place to watch a 3-D movie called It's Tough to be a Bug! It's hosted by Flik, the star of *A Bug's Life*. Most of these bugs are friendly and funny. But when the evil Hopper makes an appearance, the show gets a little bit scary.

This movie is about the tiny creatures that outnumber all others on our planet — bugs. In it, animated insects use music and special effects to show how hard their lives are. They also try to show humans just how important bugs really are. This show is much too scary for some younger kids.

The Reader Review

By: Benjamin, age 11
East Providence, RI

I am not a big fan of insects, so I found this show very suspenseful. You never know where the bugs are going to pop up next! The effects are great, right down to the Audio-Animatronics Flik and Hopper.

Pandora— The World of Avatar

Disney's Animal Kingdom has a special land called Pandora — The World of Avatar. It is a beautiful area that celebrates nature and all animal life. It has floating mountains, bridges, waterfalls, and beautiful plants — many of the plants glow at night! The area has two attractions to enjoy: Na'vi River Journey and Avatar Flight of Passage.

Avatar Flight of Passage

Who said you need wings to fly? Just climb aboard a Mountain Banshee and soar over Pandora in this exciting thrill ride. It's sure to please most kids — especially daredevils. In case you are wondering: A Mountain Banshee is a colorful flying creature that looks like a dragon. It is also known as an Ikran (say *ICK-ron*).

Meet your Avatar

Mountain Banshees don't like humans — that's why all guests need avatars (*AV-eh-tars*). Your avatar will ride the Ikran's back while you sit on something that's like a motorcycle seat. Everyone wears 3-D glasses, too.

Fly, Ikran, Fly!

As the adventure begins, the powerful creature zooms through the air — and you are along for the ride. Hang on tight! Most kids agree that this is an amazing experience — so it is very popular. Get a Fastpass if you can! You must be at least 44 inches tall to ride. If heights or motion make you feel uncomfortable, you should skip this attraction.

Na'vi River Journey

The Na'vi River Journey is a peaceful boat ride through a dark, glowing jungle. As you float on a mysterious river, be sure to notice all the details. Expect to see interesting creatures and glowing plants. You will also see (and hear) an Audio-Animatronics character called the Shaman of Song. She is gigantic! This journey is a nice way to take a cool break on a hot day.

DinoLand U.S.A.

The entrance to this land is marked by a big dinosaur skeleton. Inside, you will find life-like dinosaurs and real animals that have existed since prehistoric times. The main attraction is a ride called Dinosaur, but there are lots of other things to see and do. For a hand-clapping good time, catch Finding Nemo — The Musical. In DinoLand you can also dig for bones in a big playground, learn about real dinosaurs, or take a spin on a friendly dino ride.

Chester & Hester's Dino-Rama!

FP+

Dino-Rama is inside DinoLand U.S.A. It's a dino-themed fair, complete with carnival games and two rides. (It costs money to play the games, but you can enjoy the rides as much as you want without paying an extra penny.) Details may change in 2019.

TriceraTop Spin

The dinos that soar on this ride look like they're part of an antique wind-up toy. Just like at Dumbo the Flying Elephant and the Magic Carpets of Aladdin, riders here can control how high or low their TriceraTops go. Younger kids love this attraction.

Primeval Whirl

Speedy little cars race around the track on this mini roller coaster. Each car spins and bumps as it moves, which makes for a wild trip. You must be at least 48 inches tall to ride.

Dinosaur

This thrilling and scary ride takes guests back to the last few minutes of the Earth's Cretaceous Period. (That is when the dinosaurs died out.)

Save the dinosaur

The mission on Dinosaur is to save the last iguanodon. You have to brave a meteor shower and one of the largest Audio-Animatronics creatures Disney has ever made. It's a dinosaur called a carnotaurus, and it may be the ugliest thing you've ever seen. This monster has the face of a toad, horns like a bull, and squirrel-like arms. It looks like it's alive. The nostrils even move as it breathes. And, boy, can it run. The carnotaurus runs for about 30 feet. Be careful. This hungry monster is not just after the iguanodon — it wants to eat you, too!

An exciting (and scary) ride

Most kids agree that this is a very exciting ride, but one that might not be for everyone. Kids who don't enjoy scary rides can find some tamer dinos on TriceraTop Spin. But for kids who like to be scared, Dinosaur is a must.

You have to be at least 40 inches tall to ride Dinosaur. The ride may not be open in all of 2019.

READER TIP

"Dinosaur is very loud and dark, and it really jerks and pulls you around. Some young kids won't like it at all!"

Julia (age 11)
Prairieville, LA

Disney's Animal Kingdom

HOT TIP!

Finding Nemo — The Musical is a popular show. Plan to arrive about 30 minutes early to get a good seat.

Finding Nemo — The Musical

 FP+

Uh-oh. Nemo has wandered off *again*. Will he ever learn?! We hope not, since this show tells his story in a whole new way — with music. There are lots of peppy tunes to sing along with during the performance. High-flying acrobats, colorful puppets, and talented dancers round out the show.

The action takes place in DinoLand's Theater in the Wild. The show happens inside a building, but it seems like it's under water. You won't get wet, though, since it's all done with special effects.

The 40-minute musical show is presented several times a day. Check a park Times Guide for the schedule. It's a popular show — arrive early. The theater is air-conditioned, so you can cool off while Nemo and his friends entertain. The show is a bit long for young kids.

The Reader Review A Great Big Beautiful Day!

By: Riley, age 12
Dayton, OH

I don't love stage shows that much — but the giant fish are pretty neat! Overall, I think Finding Nemo — The Musical is best for Nemo fans.

Wilderness Explorers

In the movie *UP*, Russell is a dedicated Wilderness Explorer. He wants to earn as many merit badges as he can. Now you can become a Wilderness Explorer, too. Start by heading to Wilderness Explorer Headquarters at the Oasis bridge. After you take the official pledge, you will get field guides describing different challenges. Complete a challenge and earn a sticker badge! There are about 30 different badges in all. There is no extra charge to become an Animal Kingdom Wilderness Explorer, and the stickers are free. It's fun for the whole family.

The Boneyard

Are you ready to jump into the biggest sandbox you've ever seen? It's here, and it's filled with bones! You can uncover the bones of a mammoth and find clues about how the animal died.

There are also dinosaur footprints that roar when you jump in them and a xylophone that's made of dinosaur bones. There's a rope maze for climbing and slides to slip down, too. Be sure to check out the Olden-Gate Bridge. It looks like a dinosaur skeleton.

The Boneyard may not be open in all of 2019.

The Reader Review

By: Olivia, age 9
Watertown, WI

My brother is 5 years old and he had a better time at The Boneyard than I did. There's lots to do, but I couldn't wait to ride Dinosaur!

HOT TIP!

The xylophone is next to the trunk in The Boneyard playground. Press the bones to make a sound.

Africa

Before creating this land, Disney Imagineers spent months on the continent of Africa learning all about the plants and animals there. When they came back, they made an African forest and a grassland in Florida. Then they filled it with hundreds of the same animals they had seen in Africa. Most of the animals in Animal Kingdom came from special parks and zoos around the world. You can see many animals on a safari ride and learn all about them at Rafiki's Planet Watch.

Kilimanjaro Safaris

In this wild adventure, you ride in a vehicle that is wide open. There's almost nothing between you and the animals. You may see hippos, lions, giraffes, rhinos, elephants, and more. Some animals may even come up close. But don't worry — dangerous animals can't get near you. It is perfectly safe. You can go on a safari during the day and at night. The animals are always there.

This attraction got a new addition a few years back — zebras! Keep your eyes peeled for these beautiful creatures. And have your camera ready at all times. You can take a lot of great photos in these parts.

PHOTO BY JILL SAFRO

The Reader Review

A Great Big Beautiful Day!

By: Samuel, age 8
North Chili, NY

Kilimanjaro Safaris lets you see animals that you never thought you would see in person. I saw lions, rhinos, crocodiles, and much more! I like this ride because I want to become a scientist.

Gorilla Falls Exploration Trail

After you take a ride on the Kilimanjaro Safaris, go for a walk on the Gorilla Falls Exploration Trail. This nature trail has a lot to discover. You may come across a grazing zebra. Or spot hippos in a watering hole. And see hundreds of fish and birds in the African Aviary.

No binoculars necessary

Pick up a bird guide (they should be hanging on a post in the aviary) and see how many different birds you can spot. Afterward, make a stop at the meerkat exhibit. Some people call it the "Timon exhibit" because he's a meerkat. (There are no Pumbaas here, though. Meerkats and warthogs don't get along in real life.)

Greetings, gorillas

At the end of the trail, you see a family of gorillas. They are usually hanging out on the hills or playing. You might even spot a little gorilla in the group.

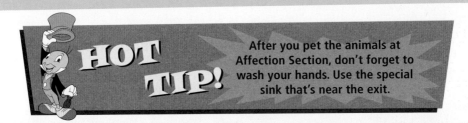

HOT TIP!

After you pet the animals at Affection Section, don't forget to wash your hands. Use the special sink that's near the exit.

Rafiki's Planet Watch

A train called the Wildlife Express is the only way to get to Rafiki's Planet Watch. (Hop aboard in Africa.) During the ride, you get a behind-the-scenes look at the buildings where animals from the safari ride are cared for.

Lend a helping hand

The exhibits at Rafiki's Planet Watch teach you what animals need to survive — and what people can do to help. There is an animal hospital, places for animals to get special care, and lots of shows meant to get you excited about conservation. There are even ways to find out about some conservation projects near your home. It's also a great place to meet Rafiki and get an autograph.

Talk to the animals

Many exhibits at Rafiki's Planet Watch are interactive. In Song of the Rainforest, you are surrounded by sounds you might hear in a real rainforest. At the Hallway of Animal Health and Care, you can sometimes watch doctors care for animals. People can walk among animals like goats and sheep in the Affection Section. It is okay to pet them, but feeding is not allowed.

Festival of the Lion King

This is one spectacular musical show. Even if you have the movie memorized, you are in for a few surprises. Many characters from the film are here, but they look a bit different. Most of them are played by humans dressed in colorful costumes.

An action-packed performance

The theater has big stages that look like parade floats. (That's because they were once used in a parade at Disneyland.) On one, Simba sits atop Pride Rock. The wisecracking Pumbaa sits on another. Gymnasts dressed like monkeys jump and do tricks.

The mighty jungle

After singers and dancers perform some of the best songs from *The Lion King*, it is time for the big finish. Stilt walkers, acrobats, and dancers join Timon for an exciting version of "The Lion Sleeps Tonight." Even the audience gets in on the act, so get ready to clap and sing along.

The Reader Review

By: Erin, age 10
Weippe, ID

The Festival of the Lion King is toe-tapping, sing-along fun for all ages. And there's acrobatics aplenty. Enjoy the show!

Who am I?

- I play the guitar.
- My family makes shoes.
- Ernesto was my idol.

Answer: Miguel

Asia

Asia is the largest continent on Earth. It's almost twice as big as North America! The land called Asia in Animal Kingdom is a lot smaller than the real thing, but it gives you an idea of what the Asian continent is like. It has jungles and rainforests and amazing animals. It's also home to the fastest raging river in Disney's Animal Kingdom. You can whirl down the river on a raft ride called Kali River Rapids. For one of the most exciting experiences of all, ride Expedition Everest. And be sure to check out the bird show called UP! —A Great Bird Adventure. It's a hoot!

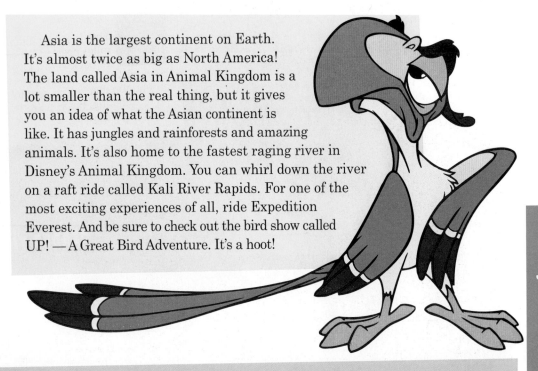

Maharajah Jungle Trek

Put on your walking shoes and keep your eyes peeled. This jungle trail is the place to spot scaly animals called Komodo dragons, plus deer, giant fruit bats (they eat melon), and tigers. You'll also see colorful birds along the way and tons of plants and trees. Pick up a map at the beginning of the trail to know what to look for.

You see the bats about halfway through your walk. Their wings are enormous! In some places, there is no glass between you and the bats. But don't worry — they're not interested in humans. Still, it might be creepy to stand so close to them. If the bats make you uncomfortable, there's a window outside the building that lets you observe them from a distance.

PHOTO BY JILL SAFRO

HIDDEN MICKEY ALERT!
The mural by the tigers is where this Mickey head is hiding.

The Reader Review

A Great Big Beautiful Day!

By: Sam, age 9
Eatontown, NJ

This is a very intense roller coaster. When you go backwards, keep your head back so you don't bounce around too much. The beginning is pretty relaxing, but you are in for some big surprises!

READER #5 RIDE PLEASER

READER TIP

"Remember to bring a water bottle with you to Animal Kingdom on hot days."

Meg (age 12)
Vero Beach, FL

DARK
Attraction Reaction

SCARY
Attraction Reaction

WILD
Attraction Reaction

FP+

Expedition Everest

Mount Everest is the tallest mountain in the world. Can you guess the name of the tallest mountain in Walt Disney World? If you said Expedition Everest, you are right! Of course, it is much more than a mountain. It's a thrilling train ride through forests and waterfalls and over snow-capped mountain peaks. This train ride is much rougher than Big Thunder Mountain. Here, you not only travel forward and backward through caverns and canyons, you also whiz by an angry yeti (that's an abominable snowman). His job is to protect the mountain from you!

This attraction is not for everyone. If you love wild, crazy, dark, and scary rides — and are at least 44 inches tall — give it a try. And be sure to say hello to the yeti for us!

Kali River Rapids

This is one of the wettest and wildest rides in Walt Disney World. (Don't bother trying to pick a dry seat on the raft, because there aren't any.) It begins as a peaceful raft trip through a rainforest. But things don't stay calm for very long. The raft bumps along down the river, spinning and turning every time it hits a wall.

Along the way you catch a glimpse of how logging (cutting down trees for lumber) can destroy the rainforest. Don't be scared if you see a fire — that's just part of the ride. You avoid the burning logs, but will you really go under that big waterfall? We won't tell. But you might want to bring a towel, just in case.

Guests must be at least 38 inches tall to ride these rapids.

PHOTO BY JILL SAFRO

Disney's Animal Kingdom

HOT TIP!

Want to keep your stuff dry while you ride Kali River Rapids? Leave it in a locker near the ride's entrance. The lockers are free for up to 2 hours.

UP! A Great Bird Adventure

Live birds are the stars of this high-flying show in the Asia section of the park. They swoop and soar and do amazing tricks. They are joined by everyone's favorite Wilderness Explorer, Russell, and his furry friend, Dug.

The show is presented several times each day. It lasts about 25 minutes. Check a park Times Guide for the schedule. And don't leave right away — sometimes a handler will bring a bird out to meet guests after the show. This great bird adventure is fun for guests of all ages.

The theater is covered, but there is no air-conditioning.

Rivers of Light

The Discovery River is home to a beautiful light show called Rivers of Light. It begins with two mystical hosts who come to the river with gifts of light. After the hosts set out on boats that look like lanterns, dancing water and light surround them. The goal is to summon animal spirits, and it works every time.

Rivers of Light is a calm way to end a busy day at the park. Check a Times Guide for the schedule. Plan to arrive at least 60 minutes early to get a seat. Better yet, ask your parents to reserve a Fastpass for each member of your family. This is a very popular show and the seats fill up quickly.

Entertainment

Don't be surprised if the performers at Animal Kingdom come right up to you. Some walk on two legs, while others walk on four — or eight. There's band music, plus drummers, live animals, and many other things to entertain you along the way. Read about some of that entertainment below.

AFRICAN ENTERTAINMENT

Drummers perform in Harambe throughout the day. There's a covered area where you can listen to them and escape the blazing sun.

Burudika

Some of Africa's finest musicians formed a band called Burudika. It is a Swahili word that means "to be refreshed." The musicians hope their pop music will make you feel refreshed. They play in Harambe. Check a park Times Guide for the Burudika show schedule.

DISCOVERY ISLAND CARNIVALE

In this street party, a music band is joined by Panchito and José Carioca (from *The Three Caballeros*). You are invited to clap and dance along. The Carnivale celebration happens every day. Check a park Times Guide for showtimes.

Di-Vine

You may think your eyes are playing tricks on you when you see this giant plant wandering through the park! The plant is actually a very talented performer walking on stilts. Her name is Di-Vine.

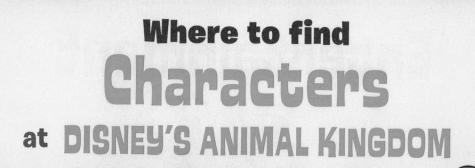

Where to find
Characters
at DISNEY'S ANIMAL KINGDOM

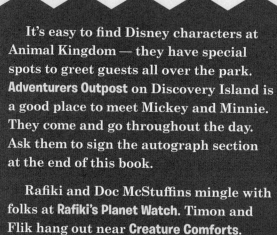

It's easy to find Disney characters at Animal Kingdom — they have special spots to greet guests all over the park. **Adventurers Outpost** on Discovery Island is a good place to meet Mickey and Minnie. They come and go throughout the day. Ask them to sign the autograph section at the end of this book.

Rafiki and Doc McStuffins mingle with folks at **Rafiki's Planet Watch**. Timon and Flik hang out near **Creature Comforts**. Look for Goofy and Pluto at **Chester & Hester's Dino-Rama** in DinoLand U.S.A. Donald likes to greet guests near the **Cretaceous Trail** in Dinoland, U.S.A. Russell and Dug welcome fans on **Discovery Island**. You could also meet Pocahontas while exploring **Discovery Island** (at Character Landing). Details may change in 2019.

Disney's Animal Kingdom

Tips

Animal Kingdom can get very hot, especially in the summer months. Head for Festival of the Lion King, Finding Nemo — The Musical, Kali River Rapids, or Rafiki's Planet Watch to cool off. And don't forget to drink lots of water.

Go to Flight of Passage, Expedition Everest, Dinosaur, and Kali River Rapids early — before they get too crowded. And try to use Fastpass.

On the Kilimanjaro Safaris ride, look at the chart over your head. The pictures will show you which animals you're about to see.

Can't find your parents? Ask the closest Disney Cast Member for help (a park worker wearing a name tag).

It doesn't really matter what time you get to the safari ride — the animals are there all day long.

It's Tough to be a Bug is very scary to some kids (especially younger ones and those who don't like the dark). In it, bugs seem to shoot quills and stinky smells, giant spiders dangle from the ceiling, and creepy critters seem to scamper beneath the seats. If you get creeped out during the show, just grab your parent and leave early.

It's fun to see how many animals you can find carved into The Tree of Life. Some folks use binoculars.

Look for Mickey and Minnie at the Adventurers Outpost on Discovery Island. Bring a phone or camera!

There is a huge mural at the entrance of Conservation Station. It is filled with animal images — and Hidden Mickeys. How many can you find?

Stash your stuff in a locker before riding Kali River Rapids — unless you don't mind if it gets wet.

Attraction Ratings

COOL
(Check It Out)

- The Oasis (the area inside the park entrance)
- Affection Section (at Rafiki's Planet Watch)
- TriceraTop Spin
- Na'vi River Journey
- Song of the Rainforest (located at Rafiki's Planet Watch)

REALLY COOL
(Don't Miss)

- The Boneyard playground
- It's Tough to be a Bug!
- UP! A Great Bird Adventure
- Maharajah Jungle Trek
- Gorilla Falls Exploration Trail
- Finding Nemo — The Musical
- Rivers of Light

THE COOLEST
(See at least twice)

- Expedition Everest
- Avatar: Flight of Passage
- Kilimanjaro Safaris
- Kali River Rapids
- Festival of the Lion King
- Dinosaur
- Primeval Whirl

Your favorite Disney's Animal Kingdom attractions

_____

_____

_____

_____

_____

_____

Everything Else in the World

No matter what you're interested in — water fun, sports, or animals — Walt Disney World has enough to make every minute of your vacation a blast. After you visit the theme parks, there's still so much to do. There are water parks, speedy boats to rent, horses to ride, fish to catch, and lots of neat shopping spots.

If you are into sports, you may want to check out the ESPN Wide World of Sports Complex, rent a bike, or try some miniature golf. To test your detective skills, join one of Walt Disney World's special scavenger hunts.

In this chapter, you can read up on all the extra activities and find out about hotels and restaurants at Walt Disney World. Then you can help your family decide where to stay, where to eat, and what to do when you're not at the theme parks.

Waters of the World

It's easy to get wet, stay cool, and have fun at Walt Disney World. That's because it's a water wonderland. Choose a water park or take a dip in your hotel pool. (If you're under the age of 14 and you want to visit a water park, you must go with a guest who is older than 14.)

Typhoon Lagoon

A typhoon is a powerful, windy storm. It dumps huge amounts of rain and sends objects flying through the air. This water park looks like a typhoon hit it. There's even a boat stuck on a mountaintop! Of course, a storm didn't really put the boat there — Disney Imagineers did. They also put in pools, waterslides, and a raft ride.

Catch the wave

The big pool here is like a small ocean. It has 6-foot waves! That makes body-surfing tons of fun. There are speed slides to try, too. In the mood for a thrill? Try Crush 'n' Gusher. It's like a water roller coaster. For a calmer experience, you can hop into a tube and float along a lazy river. There's also a special area just for younger kids — Ketchakiddee Creek. It has small slides and other games.

Miss Adventure Falls

There's an exciting new ride in town. Miss Adventure Falls is a wild water ride for the whole family — up to 4 people can travel in one raft. It's the longest ride ever built at a Walt Disney World water park. During the 2-minute splashy trip, you'll spy lots of sparkly treasures. Hold on tight! And keep your eyes out for a treasure-hunting parrot.

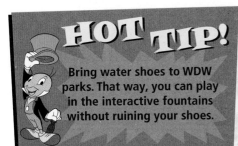

HOT TIP!

Bring water shoes to WDW parks. That way, you can play in the interactive fountains without ruining your shoes.

Blizzard Beach

Would you wear a swimsuit to a snow-covered mountain? Probably not. But you should wear one to Blizzard Beach. It looks like a place to ski, but it's really a water park. So don't worry if you can't ski. Nobody skis down the mountain here. They slide!

Reach the peak

Like a real ski resort, all the action centers around a mountain. In this case, it is Mount Gushmore. To get to the top, you can take a chairlift. The ride gives you a great view of the park. The scariest slide on the mountain is Summit Plummet. It begins 120 feet in the air, on a platform that looks like a ski jump. It drops you down a steep slide at about 60 miles per hour. That's faster than many cars go on the highway. You must be at least 48 inches tall to ride Summit Plummet.

Slip-sliding away

There are plenty of other ways to slide down the mountain. Tube slides, body slides, and inner-tube rides can keep you busy all day long. It's fun to splash in the wave pool, too. For preteens, there's Ski Patrol Training Camp, with its "iceberg" obstacle course and ropes for swinging into the water. Tike's Peak is a special place for younger kids. It has slides and a snow-castle fountain play area.

READER TIP

"Go to a water park early in the day — when it's hot and crowded at the theme parks. Then you can return to the theme park when it cools down in the evening."

David (age 14)
Calabasas, CA

Everything Else in the World

Fort Wilderness

Fort Wilderness is tucked away in a woodland area of Walt Disney World. (It isn't really a fort. It's a campground.) You can stay overnight or just come for a day. There are tennis and volleyball courts, and a marina with lots of boats. You could spend days here and not run out of things to do. If you have a bit of time, you could stop in at the pony farm or rent a boat for a ride around Bay Lake and the Seven Seas Lagoon.

Pony Farm

There is a small farm at Fort Wilderness. It's a short walk from Pioneer Hall. There is no charge to visit the farm, but it costs $8 to go for a pony ride. Be sure to bring a grown-up with you. If you don't want to ride a pony, you can still stop by and say hello. Most visitors think a trip to the farm is a fun way to spend some time away from the parks. Kids must weigh less than 80 pounds and be no taller than 48 inches to ride. They also have to be able to hold on by themselves.

More Fort Wilderness Fun

Fort Wilderness offers lots of other things to do. You can rent a canoe for a trip along some canals. Or you can rent a bicycle and explore one of the many trails. At the Tri-Circle-D Ranch, you can see the horses that pull the trolleys in the Magic Kingdom. (They live in a barn near Pioneer Hall.)

Kids older than age 9 can take a trail ride on horseback. You can also enjoy a wagon ride, go fishing, or roast marshmallows at a campfire with Chip and Dale.

Sports

Kids who like sports can find plenty of ways to keep active at Walt Disney World. You can rent boats and bikes at one of the resorts, or play miniature golf on one of Disney's themed courses. To see athletes at work, visit the ESPN Wide World of Sports complex. Read on to find out how.

Speed Boats

A Sea Raycer is a speedy little motorboat that you can rent. And it delivers big thrills. If you are at least 12 years old and 5 feet tall, you can drive one yourself.

These zippy boat rides get very high marks from kids. The boat goes surprisingly fast and the ride can be bumpy, especially if you drive over a wave caused by another boat. So hang on tight. And drive carefully — there is a lot of traffic out there. Stay far away from other boats.

You can rent a Sea Raycer at many Disney resorts. The cost is about $32 for a half hour.

ESPN Wide World of Sports Complex

Major sports nuts might enjoy a visit to this complex. It has facilities for every sport you can imagine. The Atlanta Braves baseball team comes here for spring training (in March).

You can spend a day watching some amateur events. Tickets to the complex cost about $14 for kids ages 3 to 9 and about $19 for anyone 10 or older. If you want to see a professional game, you have to buy your tickets ahead of time. The prices vary. Have a parent call 407-939-4263 for information or to buy tickets.

Miniature Golf

Even if you've never held a golf club before, you may enjoy mini-golf. It's fun to play and full of surprises.

Fantasia Gardens

If you have seen the old movie *Fantasia*, you'll know how this miniature golf course got its name. Where else will you find hippos on tiptoe, dancing mushrooms, or xylophone stairs?

The holes are grouped by musical themes. At the Dance of the Hours hole, watch the hippopotamus standing on an alligator. If you hit a golf ball through the gator's mouth, the hippo dances!

The cost is about $12 to play one round for kids ages 3 to 9 and about $14 for anyone 10 or older.

Disney's Winter Summerland

Sometimes even Santa Claus needs a vacation. Just like you, he picked Walt Disney World as the perfect place to go and have fun.

As the story goes, Santa and his helpers built these mini-golf courses as a place to relax and enjoy the sun. That's why one looks like a beach, with sand castles and surfboards on it. But then the elves got homesick, so they built a second course that reminded them of the North Pole. Everything looks like it is covered in snow. There are even igloos, jolly snowmen, and holes for ice fishing.

For a bit of a challenge, try the summer course. It's a little harder than the winter course. Santa is snoozing at one of the trickiest holes. You have to hit the ball across his belly without waking him up. The winter holes offer surprises, too. Get the ball in one of the holes and Mickey himself pops out of a present!

To play on one course, it costs about $12 for kids ages 3 to 9 and about $14 for anyone 10 or older.

Scavenger Hunts

If you are a fan of the tales told by Walt Disney World's shows and rides, you'll probably enjoy these special tours. Each one makes you feel like you are part of the story.

Family Magic Tour

This program is fun for the whole family. Parents and kids can join in a themed scavenger hunt through the Magic Kingdom. Guests search for the answers to different clues that lead to the missing item.

If you go on this two-hour tour, be sure to wear your sneakers — you will be doing lots of walking! The cost is about $39 for each person age 3 and over. Parents can use the My Disney Experience app or website, or call 407-WDW-TOUR (939-8687) to make reservations.

Pirate Adventure

Did you know that there is pirates' treasure buried at Walt Disney World? Some is hidden somewhere around Crescent Lake. (That's a lake near Epcot's World Showcase.) Every morning, a cruise for kids sails out from the Yacht Club resort in search of it.

The Caribbean Beach resort has a special pirate adventure, too.

Do you think you are up to the challenge of a treasure hunt? The captain of the ship will give you a map and a series of clues to help you on your way. During the journey, all junior pirates get to enjoy a drink and a snack.

You will have two hours to find the hidden treasure. If you do, it is yours to keep! Cruises take place each morning and are for kids ages 4 to 12. The cost is about $49 per child. Cruises happen every day, but they may be cancelled if the weather is bad. To make reservations, your parents can call 407-939-3463 or visit *www.mydisneyexperience.com*.

Disney Springs

What WDW spot has shops and restaurants, movies, games, and much more? Disney Springs! There are lots of areas for kids to explore and things to discover — like mechanical dinosaurs and cars that are also boats. Many spots offer live entertainment. Pick up a Times Guide for the schedule. (You can get one at Guest Relations.) There are four different neighborhoods at Disney Springs: The West Side, The Landing, The Marketplace, and Town Center (a shopping mall area).

The West Side

This zone has places to shop, eat, go bowling (at a place called Splitsville), catch a movie, and listen to live music. It also has a big balloon that takes guests for rides in the sky (you'll need a ticket and a grown-up to ride with you).

The Landing

This neighborhood has waterside shops and snack spots. It's also where the Amphicars are. (That is one of them in the photo above.)

Marketplace

Searching for a souvenir? Be sure to visit the Marketplace. There are lots of shops there. One spot that kids love is World of Disney. It's packed with Disney-themed goodies. The Once Upon a Toy store has a design your own Mr. Potato Head station. You can also make a wacky creation at the Lego store. (It's okay just to play — you don't have to buy.)

HIDDEN MICKEY ALERT!
Some of the Marketplace's dancing water fountains form the shape of you-know-who!

Electrical Water Pageant

Have you ever seen a parade on a lake? Now is your chance. The Electrical Water Pageant is Disney's floating parade. The pageant made its magical debut in October 1971. It was part of the grand opening of the Polynesian Village Resort. Walt Disney World was three weeks old at the time.

Above the sea

The water parade takes place on The Seven Seas Lagoon (the lake next to the Magic Kingdom) and on Bay Lake (behind the Contemporary Resort hotel). The nightly show has thousands of sparkling lights on connected floats. The floats have screens that show King Triton and other sea creatures — turtles, sea horses, an octopus, and a sea serpent. It's all set to Disney music. The pageant may be cancelled when the weather is stormy.

The end of the parade is a tribute to America. That's when the lights turn into flags and stars. The finale has a patriotic music medley, too. If you know the words to "You're a Grand Old Flag" and "Yankee Doodle Dandy," feel free to sing along.

Catch it if you can!

You can view the Electrical Water Pageant from many locations around Bay Lake and the Seven Seas Lagoon. Here is the schedule:
- Polynesian Village Resort — about 9 P.M.
- Grand Floridian Resort — about 9:15 P.M.
- Wilderness Lodge — about 9:30 P.M.
- Fort Wilderness Resort and Campground — about 9:45 P.M.
- Contemporary Resort — about 10:10 P.M. (When the Magic Kingdom's fireworks take place at 10 P.M., the Water Pageant begins soon after the fireworks end.)
- Right outside the entrance of the Magic Kingdom park — 10:35 P.M. (On nights when the Magic Kingdom is open late.) Details may change.

Walt Disney World Resorts

There are more than 25 different resort hotels on Walt Disney World property. There are so many hotel rooms that you could stay in a different one every night for 68 years! Just like the rides at the parks, each of the resorts has its own special theme. And all of the resorts are fun to stay at. But they are fun to visit, too. So if you have time, you might want to stop by some of them — to have a meal or just to enjoy the atmosphere.

Resorts near the Magic Kingdom

Contemporary

This was the first-ever Walt Disney World hotel. It looked very modern when it was built in 1971 (that's how it got its name). When it opened, it had a talking elevator and a monorail station right in the middle of it. It still has the monorail today, plus an arcade and Chef Mickey's — a fun place to have a meal and mingle with Mickey and his pals.

Contemporary Tip

In the center of the resort is a 3-sided mural that's 90 feet tall. There are colorful pictures of children and animals all over it. One of the goats has five legs. See how long it takes you to find him!

Fort Wilderness

Stay in a camper, tent, or cabin at this pretty wooded campground. This resort has many activities. You can go for a wagon ride, visit a pony farm, or take a trip through the woods on a horse. At night, Chip and Dale sometimes roast marshmallows by a campfire. This is also home to a popular dinner show called the Hoop-Dee-Doo Musical Revue.

Fort Wilderness Tip

The horses that pull trolleys in the Magic Kingdom live in a stable at Fort Wilderness. You can visit for free — and maybe even see them getting new shoes from the blacksmith.

Grand Floridian

This elegant hotel looks like a huge mansion from the early 1900s. At first, it seems to be for adults, but it's also fun for kids. There may be activities like storytelling and crafts. Or you can sit in a comfy chair and listen to a band play in the lobby. There are two pools: one is surrounded by roses and the other has a waterfall. There is an Alice in Wonderland splash zone, too. The monorail has a station here.

> **Grand Floridian Tip**
>
> At Christmastime, the Grand Floridian lobby is home to a giant gingerbread house. It's made of real gingerbread — and so big that grown-up people can fit inside!

The Monorail

The monorail connects the Magic Kingdom with the Contemporary, Polynesian Village, and Grand Floridian resorts. It's also a great way to get from the Magic Kingdom to Epcot — just switch monorail trains at the Transportation and Ticket Center.

PHOTO BY JILL SAFRO

Polynesian Village

The plants and trees at this hotel make it look like a tropical island. The greenery and cheery colors in the main building make the setting seem real even when you're indoors. There's a pool that looks like it is made from lava from a volcano, and a beach to relax on. The WDW monorail makes a stop here, too.

> **Polynesian Tip**
>
> Grab a snack (and your family) and have a dessert picnic on or near the beach. Then enjoy the fireworks over the Magic Kingdom — the show's music plays all around you!

Wilderness Lodge

With its log columns and totem poles, this hotel looks like a national park from the American Northwest. The fireplaces and rocking chairs in the main building make you feel right at home. There is an indoor stream and a bridge. Outside, there's an erupting geyser and a pool. There are so many Hidden Mickeys here that there's a tour and contest to see how many you can find.

> **Wilderness Lodge Tip**
>
> Look for the "Proterozoic Fossils and Minerals" display. It's a key to the rocky strata of the giant Grand Canyon fireplace in the main lobby.

Resorts near Epcot and Disney's Hollywood Studios

BoardWalk

This hotel is designed to look the way Atlantic City, New Jersey, once did. Just like on an old-fashioned boardwalk, there are games and snack stands here for everyone to enjoy. You can rent a special bicycle built for four or swim in a pool that looks like an amusement park.

BoardWalk Tip

Look for a crystal globe under a chandelier in the main building. It is a time capsule that will be opened on Walt Disney World's 50th anniversary — October 1, 2021.

Port Orleans — French Quarter

The special details at this hotel make it look like New Orleans, Louisiana. There's a long river and a fun pool with a curving dragon water slide.

French Quarter Tip

After taking a dip in the French Quarter pool, you might want to check out the pool at Port Orleans Riverside. You can get there by walking or taking a Walt Disney World bus. Be sure to take your parents with you!

Caribbean Beach

Happy and colorful, this hotel looks like resorts on some Caribbean islands. You can have fun in the sun all day at its beaches, pools, and playgrounds. A bunch of the rooms here have a pirate theme. And there is a cool, interactive splash area and slide at the pool.

Caribbean Beach Tip

The hotel has a bike path that circles a lake. It's more than a mile long! Bikes can be rented at the marina.

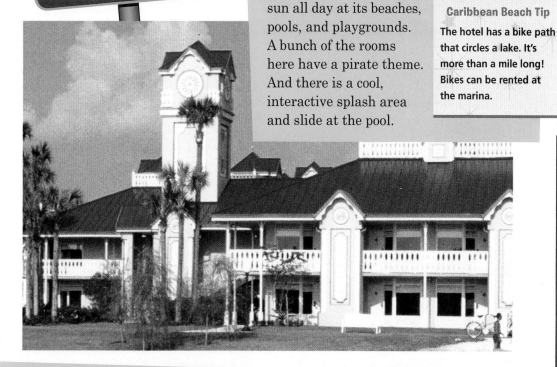

Port Orleans — Riverside

This hotel's buildings look like mansions and country homes from the Old South. The food court is designed after a cotton mill, and it has a water-wheel that is 30 feet tall. The pool is on Ol' Man Island, an area that was inspired by the story of Tom Sawyer.

Riverside Tip

If you like to fish, head down to the Fishin' Hole at Ol' Man Island. The resort has poles to rent and worms to buy.

Old Key West

The town houses that make up this resort have all the comforts of home. The palm trees and sunny design make it a very warm and welcoming place. And the pool has an awesome slide!

Old Key West Tip

Kids of all ages enjoy the crafts and games at Community Hall and the wet and wild games at the main pool.

Pop Century Resort

The twentieth century might be over, but it is hard to forget when you visit this hotel. Giant icons (like old cell phones and jukeboxes) decorate the buildings. The hotel pays tribute to each decade from the 1950s to the 1990s.

Pop Century Tip

On hot days, cool off by splashing around in the hotel's interactive fountains.

Swan and Dolphin

You can't miss the dolphin and swan statues that sit on top of these hotels — they are gigantic. There's lots to do at the Swan and Dolphin. The pool area is a ton of fun. And you can walk or take a boat to Epcot, Disney's Hollywood Studios, and the BoardWalk resort from here.

Swan and Dolphin Tip

There are 250 swan and dolphin statues at this resort. Some are big, but some are very small. See how many you can spot.

Saratoga Springs Resort

This hotel is designed to look like upstate New York in the late 1800s. There are lots of pretty gardens to look at. But the best views come from a special lakeside spot. From there you can see the lights of Disney Springs. The pools here are a blast!

Saratoga Springs Tip

The pool area has a special water-spray play area with lots of squirting fountains. It's just for kids!

PHOTO BY JILL SAFRO

Yacht and Beach Club

These two connected hotels are meant to look like the homes near the beaches of Massachusetts. Even the pool makes it feel as if you're at the beach — the bottom is covered with sand.

Yacht and Beach Club Tip

Pack walking shoes. One of the cool parts about staying here is that you can walk to Epcot, Disney's Hollywood Studios, and BoardWalk.

Art of Animation

This resort is a celebration of animation. So if you are a fan of *The Little Mermaid*, *The Lion King*, *Finding Nemo*, and *Cars*, you are going to love it here. Be sure to look up — there are tons of giant character statues. Super cool!

Art of Animation Tip

Kids love the pools at this resort. Don't miss the awesome splash zone in the Finding Nemo Courtyard. It's a great place to have fun with a younger brother or sister.

Resorts near Animal Kingdom

All-Star Resorts

There are three All-Star resorts, and each one of them has a special theme — sports, music, or movies. It's easy to tell which All-Star you are visiting because they

All-Star Tip

There are a whole lot of Hidden Mickeys to hunt for. Start your search at the main statue in each of the resorts.

have giant icons that are even bigger than the buildings. At All-Star Music, look for big cowboy boots. A huge football helmet means you are at All-Star Sports. And when you see a 38-foot-tall Buzz Lightyear, there's no doubt you're at All-Star Movies.

Coronado Springs

The land at this hotel looks like parts of the southwestern United States and Mexico. The buildings are the color of clay. There's a pool that looks like an ancient pyramid, with a slide that passes under a spitting jaguar. Beside it is a sandbox with ancient treasures waiting to be uncovered.

Coronado Springs Tip

The resort has a play area called The Explorers Zone. It is designed to look like Aztec ruins. Kids ages 2 to 12 may enjoy its slides, jungle gym, and dig site.

Everything Else in the World

Animal Kingdom Lodge

Creatures like giraffes, zebras, gazelles, and beautiful birds live near this hotel — and they are all real. The trees and animals make it seem as if the resort is set in an African savanna. A giant mud fireplace and thatched roofs add to the feeling that you really are in Africa.

Animal Kingdom Lodge Tip

Almost all of the rooms have excellent views of the animals. But if you want an even closer look, remember to bring a pair of binoculars from home.

Movies Under the Stars

There are lots of fun things for kids to enjoy at Walt Disney World resorts. One of them is called Movies Under the Stars. Each night, a different animated film is shown outdoors. Sometimes there's a campfire and marshmallow roast before the show. You can get a movie schedule at your hotel's front desk. (The movie may be moved indoors or cancelled if the weather is bad.)

HOT TIP!

Movies Under the Stars are extra special at Disney's Fort Wilderness resort — Chip and Dale often stop by to say hello before the movie begins!

Restaurants

Eating at Walt Disney World can be as much fun as riding Splash Mountain (well, almost as much fun!). Here are our suggestions for the best spots in each theme park to head to for your favorite foods.

Magic Kingdom
Best Places for Favorite Foods

Candy and crispie treats . . . . Main Street Confectionery

Chicken nuggets . . . . Cosmic Ray's Starlight Cafe

Cookies . . . . Main Street Confectionery

Fruit . . . . Liberty Square Market

Hamburgers . . . . Cosmic Ray's Starlight Cafe

Hot dogs . . . . Casey's Corner

Ice cream . . . . Plaza Ice Cream Parlor

LeFou's Brew (apple slush drink) . . . . Gaston's Tavern

Macaroni and cheese . . . . Columbia Harbour House

Pizza . . . . Pinocchio Village Haus

Pretzels . . . . Fantasyland Pretzel Stand (in Storybook Circus)

Smoothies . . . . Main Street Bakery

Turkey legs . . . . Frontierland Turkey Leg Cart

Veggie burgers . . . . Cosmic Ray's Starlight Cafe

Epcot
Best Places for Favorite Foods

Candy and cookies . . . . Karamell-Küche (in Germany)

Chicken nuggets . . . . Electric Umbrella (in Future World)

Egg rolls . . . . Lotus Blossom Cafe (in China)

Fruit . . . . Sunshine Seasons (in The Land)

Hamburgers . . . . Electric Umbrella (in Future World)

Ice cream . . . . L'Artisan des Glaces (in France)

Macaroni and cheese . . . . Sunshine Seasons (in The Land)

Pasta with tomato sauce . . . . Liberty Inn (in The American Adventure)

Pastries . . . . Les Halles Boulangerie Patisserie (in France)

Peanut butter and jelly sandwiches . . . . Sunshine Seasons (in The Land)

Pizza . . . . Via Napoli (in Italy)

Smoothies . . . . Fountain View Espresso & Bakery (in Future World)

Soft pretzels . . . . The Pretzel Wagon (in Germany)

Tacos . . . . La Cantina de San Angel (in Mexico)

Disney's Hollywood Studios
Best Places for Favorite Foods

Chicken and waffles . . . . The Backlot Express

Chicken noodle soup . . . . Sci-Fi Dine-In Theater

Chicken nuggets . . . . ABC Commissary

Fruit . . . . Anaheim Produce (in the Sunset Ranch Market)

Grilled cheese . . . . Woody's Lunch Box (in Toy Story Land)

Hamburgers . . . . Backlot Express

Hot dogs . . . . Fairfax Fare (in the Sunset Ranch Market)

Ice cream . . . . Hollywood Scoops (in the Sunset Ranch Market)

Macaroni and cheese . . . . Hollywood and Vine

Milk shakes . . . . 50's Prime Time Cafe

Peanut butter and jelly sandwiches . . . . ABC Commissary

Pizza . . . . PizzeRizzo

Smoothies . . . . Trolley Car Cafe

Spaghetti . . . . Mama Melrose's Ristorante Italiano

HOT TIP!

Most Disney restaurants have special menus for kids. Just ask!

Disney's Animal Kingdom
Best Places for Favorite Foods

Barbecued ribs and chicken .... Flame Tree Barbecue

Candy .... Chester and Hester's Dinosaur Treasures

Chicken nuggets and fries .... Restaurantosaurus

Cookies .... Kusafiri Coffee Shop and Bakery

Corn dogs .... Famous Sausages (in Harambe Market)

Egg rolls .... Yak and Yeti Local Food Cafes

Fruit .... Harambe Fruit Market

Grilled cheese .... Rainforest Cafe

Hamburgers .... Restaurantosaurus

Hot dogs .... Restaurantosaurus

Ice cream .... Anandapur Ice Cream Truck

Pizza .... Pizzafari

Smoothies .... Creature Comforts

Veggie burgers. .... Rainforest Cafe

Eating with Disney Characters

Kids of all ages enjoy eating with the characters. It's one of the best ways to see your favorite Disney stars. They will come right up to your table to meet you. Bring a camera because the characters are also happy to pose for photos. And don't forget your pen so you can collect some autographs.

Each of the theme parks has at least one restaurant that invites the characters over. Many of the resorts have character meals, too. They are very popular, so no matter which restaurant your family chooses, it's a good idea to make reservations far ahead of time. Ask a parent to call 407-WDW-DINE (939-3463).

Character meals aren't fun just because you get to see the characters. They are also special because the food is yummy! Picky eaters may prefer one of the buffets — with so much to choose from, you are sure to find something you will like.

Dinner Shows

Hoop-Dee-Doo Musical Revue

Entertainers sing, dance, and tell jokes while you chow down on chicken, ribs, and veggies. The jokes are silly, but everyone always has a good time. That's probably why the Hoop-Dee-Doo is the most popular dinner show in Walt Disney World!

Mickey's Backyard Barbecue

Mickey's having a barbecue, and you are welcome to join the fun. You can eat all the chicken, hamburgers, hot dogs, barbecued ribs, and dessert you want, while a live band plays country music. There's also a show for kids, games, and dancing with the Disney characters.

The Spirit of Aloha

Aloha! That means "hello" (and "good-bye") in Hawaiian. You'll hear it a lot at this show. Performers do the hula and other Hawaiian dances while servers dish out Polynesian food.

Reservations for all of these shows should be made before you arrive at Walt Disney World. A parent can call 407-WDW-DINE (939-3463), or visit *www.mydisneyexperience.com*.

MAGICAL MEMORIES

The fun doesn't have to end when your vacation does. Use these pages to preserve your Disney memories.

These are the people I vacationed with:

I arrived at Walt Disney World on:

_____
(month/day/year)

I stayed for _____ days.

My first day at Walt Disney World I went to:

I traveled to Walt Disney World by:
[ ] car
[ ] plane
[ ] bus
[ ] boat
[ ] train

The name of our hotel was:

I went on this ride first:

My usual bedtime is _____ o'clock.

During my trip, the latest I went to bed was _____ o'clock.

The earliest I woke up was _____ o'clock.

Draw your favorite
Disney character here!

The weather at
Walt Disney World was:
[ ] sunny
[ ] rainy
[ ] windy
[ ] chilly
[ ] snowy

This attraction
wasn't what
I expected:

It surprised me
because it was:

The scariest ride I went on was:

My favorite ride was:

I went on it _____ times.

Tape a used
Walt Disney World
ticket or a receipt here!

If I were an Imagineer,
this is the ride
I would design:

My least favorite
ride was:

I didn't like it
because it was:

MAGICAL MEMORIES

The best Disney theme park was:

[ ] Magic Kingdom

[ ] Epcot

[ ] Disney's Hollywood Studios

[ ] Disney's Animal Kingdom

Vacations aren't just fun; they're educational, too! One thing that I learned at Walt Disney World is:

My favorite restaurant was:

I ate:

Building a theme park was Walt Disney's dream. What's your dream?

The funniest thing that happened at Walt Disney World was:

Tape a Walt Disney World vacation photo here!

I found _____ Hidden Mickeys.

The best
Walt Disney World
snack is:

I met _____ characters
during my vacation.

The first character I saw was:

Tape the corner of a
Walt Disney World
napkin here!

Tape a
Walt Disney World
receipt here!

It's fun to remember a vacation with souvenirs.
One souvenir I brought back is:

My favorite character is:

Someday, I'll go back to Walt Disney World.
The first thing I'll do when I get there is:

AUTOGRAPHS

Disney characters love to sign autographs. Bring a pen and ask them to sign these pages for you. Have a parent snap a picture and tape it beside the autograph. That will help you remember the magical moment!

Mickey Mouse

Mickey and me!
(tape photo here)

AUTOGRAPHS

Minnie Mouse

Minnie and me!
(tape photo here)